A PILGRIM'S INTER-FAITH GUIDE TO THE HOLY LAND

FRANKLIN H. LITTELL

with the assistance of
MARCIA SACHS LITTELL

A PILGRIM'S INTER-FAITH GUIDE TO THE HOLY LAND

CARTA & THE JERUSALEM POST

ISBN 965 220 030 1

Printed in Israel

CONTENTS

INTRODUCTION

Israel is today a sacred area to four religions of divine revelation: Judaism, Christianity, Islam and Baha'i. For Judaism, Jerusalem is the city of King David and the site of the First and Second Temples. The other major sacred cities are Safad, Hebron and Tiberias. For Christianity, the key locations are Jerusalem, Bethlehem and Nazareth. Islam is linked to Jerusalem by the "further mosque," El Aksa, after Mecca and Medina the most sacred shrine of the religion founded by Muhammed. The international headquarters of the Baha'i faith are in Haifa, near the shrine of the founder of the movement; the shrine of the forerunner is located just outside Acre.

Of course "the Holy Land," as it has been called for centuries, once comprised a greater territory than the present State of Israel. Solomon's kingdom included land that is today governed by regimes in Lebanon, Syria and Jordan. Israel as a political entity — like other states carved out of the former Ottoman Empire — is a product of the territorial settlements following World Wars I and II. As a religious entity, however, its claim to life is much older. That ancient claim, based upon the Scriptures (cf. Gen. 15:5, 18; 26:3), was reaffirmed by the work and sacrifice of pioneers long before the Balfour Declaration (2 November 1917) and a formal Resolution of the United Nations (29 November 1947) gave it standing in international affairs.

Since independence the young nation has come through four intense battles for survival (1948, 1956, 1967, 1973), each involving great cost in lives and economic wealth. The four assaults, like the Nazi war against the Jews that produced the Holocaust, have been given ideological or religious justification by modern crusaders who secularize religion and sacralize politics. All the more remarkable, therefore, is Israel's careful stewardship of the religious shrines of all four faiths — even faiths some of whose spokesmen have advocated the destruction of the nation and a second mass slaughter of Jews. In the same spirit Israel, as a republic, protects the political rights of the several Marxist sects — even though Marxist as well as fascist governments have trained and armed the forces that have repeatedly attacked her people by terrorism or open military assault.

Although pilgrims from abroad usually do not realize it, because services are generally good and morale so evident, all but one of the governments neighbouring Israel have had declarations of war against her since 1948. The exception, Egypt, first took the path of peace in 1977.

The faithful of Judaism, Christianity, Islam and Baha'ism now enjoy, under the custodianship of the Israel government, for the first time in their entire histories, immediate and unimpeded access to their holy places and houses of worship. More than that, the government of Israel gives substantial financial support to the repair and upkeep of the major shrines of all resident faiths. This is no mean task, since centuries of religious bigotry and warring have made religious antagonism one of the most explosive forces in the Near East.

Even with careful Israeli police protection, bookstores or cemeteries or academies are occasionally damaged by zealots from Jewish or Christian or Muslim sects. But such incidents are at least as rare in an Israeli city as they are in — let us say — Lincoln, Nebraska or Hannover, West Germany or Manchester, England. In fact, even during the high holy days of the three militant faiths, when overseas pilgrims add their anticipation and excitement to the electric atmosphere of the Holy Land, under Israeli police protection both persons and shrines are more secure from violence than ever before.

The major sites here called to the visitor's attention represent in a certain sense an arbitrary selection. The Holy Land is full of hundreds of places and scenes worthy of the pilgrim's attention. But most pilgrims have time only to visit a few, and they miss some of the most impressive scenes because the usual guidebook is too large and too detailed to be helpful in making a practical list of real possibilities.

The sites here listed and described were selected for several reasons. First, choice was made of places worthy of the attention of any intelligent traveller, regardless of his own religious persuasion. The perspective is — in the broadest sense — ecumenical. Second, choice was made of sites impressive for their present concrete impact on the viewer. The plain where the sun is said to have stood still during Joshua's battle (Josh. 10:12) looks very much like other stretches of the Valley of Aijalon, but there is only one Masada in the world. Third, the choice was limited to a number which the average tourist could manage in a stay of two or three weeks. With one exception, the sites are readily accessible by inexpensive public transportation or by foot.

Finally, the *Pilgrim's Guide to the Holy Land* provides a number of aids to make the cities and the countryside more intelligible. Israel is a nation profoundly conscious of history. Not only is its map dotted with hundreds of place names which evoke the memories of the student of the Scriptures: there are dozens of *kibbutzim* and *moshavim* and city streets more recently named for the great men and women of the past and present ages. As the visitor goes between major shrines, or visits friends and relatives, he will find it interesting to note who has been memorialized.

To the Jew and Christian, Jerusalem is the Holy City — the "navel of the world," as the fathers called it. A preponderance of sites is found in this city — Jerusalem the Golden, a city set on a hill. Therefore supplementary maps and lists reflect Jerusalem's precedence among the cities of the monotheistic faiths. Therefore — and this is more important yet! — pilgrims of other faiths may join with overseas Jews in saying in anticipation, and on the day they depart affirming with determination, "Next year in Jerusalem!"

Franklin H. Littell

MAJOR SITES AND SHRINES

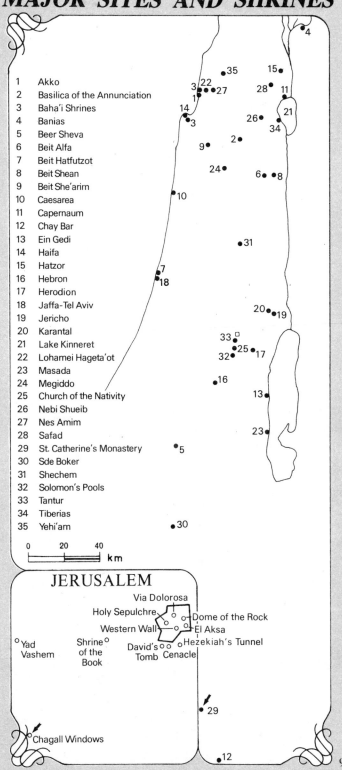

1   Akko
2   Basilica of the Annunciation
3   Baha'i Shrines
4   Banias
5   Beer Sheva
6   Beit Alfa
7   Beit Hatfutzot
8   Beit Shean
9   Beit She'arim
10 Caesarea
11 Capernaum
12 Chay Bar
13 Ein Gedi
14 Haifa
15 Hatzor
16 Hebron
17 Herodion
18 Jaffa-Tel Aviv
19 Jericho
20 Karantal
21 Lake Kinneret
22 Lohamei Hageta'ot
23 Masada
24 Megiddo
25 Church of the Nativity
26 Nebi Shueib
27 Nes Amim
28 Safad
29 St. Catherine's Monastery
30 Sde Boker
31 Shechem
32 Solomon's Pools
33 Tantur
34 Tiberias
35 Yehi'am

0   20   40
├───┼───┼───┼───┤ k m

JERUSALEM

Via Dolorosa
Holy Sepulchre
Western Wall
Dome of the Rock
El Aksa
Hezekiah's Tunnel
David's Tomb   Cenacle

Yad Vashem

Shrine of the Book

Chagall Windows

9

JERUSALEM
INTRODUCTION

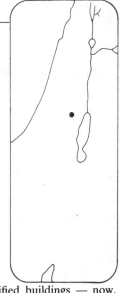

Going up to Jerusalem from the Mediterranean coast, or more abruptly from the Jordan Valley, leaves an indelible impression on the mind. Jerusalem is truly a city set on a hill.

One of the most memorable experiences is to search out a high point in the high city (750 metres above sea level, 1,142 metres above the Dead Sea). From the height, the pilgrim with a good map° can identify many of the sites before setting forth. A convenient place to find such a panoramic view is the top of the tower of the Y.M.C.A. on King David Street. On each of the four sides of the parapet are metal plates with skyline and identified buildings — now, with the rapid building of recent years, out of date but still useful. Alternative facilities open to the public, with magnificent views of the city, are the tower of the Church of the Redeemer in the Old City (dedicated in 1898 by German Emperor Wilhelm II) and the tower of the Russian Orthodox compound on the Mount of Olives (built during the reign of Tsar Alexander III, who also personally sponsored construction of the Church of Mary Magdelene in the Garden of Gethsemane below).

Another recommended initial experience is to visit the large model of ancient Jerusalem (at the time of the Second Temple) on the grounds of the Holyland Hotel in Bayit V'Gan. Here one can see, in a striking — if somewhat

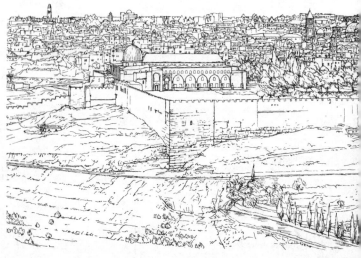

idealized — form, what the "Old City" looked like before it was ravaged and defiled by the Roman conquerors when they suppressed Jewish revolts in 68–70 of the Common Era. By use of a convenient *Pictorial Guide*, sold on the premises, a number of locations can be identified which are still subject to view.

Until little more than a century ago, the mixed Jewish and Muslim and Christian population of Jerusalem was still concentrated within the walls of what is now called "the Old City." In the 1860s, on the initiative of the philanthropist Sir Moses Montefiore, the first Jewish settlements were established outside the walls (beginning with the section easily identified today by the windmill and Montefiore Memorial). Since reunification of the city following the Israeli victory in 1967 ("the Six-Day War"), there has been a tremendous expansion of building and many new suburbs have been created.

Nevertheless, the chief sites of the Old City and the new city are within easy walking distance of each other. The same can be said of the immediate outlying districts: Mount Zion, the Valley of Hinnom, the Kidron Valley, Gethsemane and the Mount of Olives; Yemin Moshe, Rehavia, Givat Ram, Mea She'arim, Morasha and the American Colony. Most of the inner city, like the new suburbs, has been built of the beautiful native stone. Green areas and parks abound. Walking, the pilgrim's proper locomotion, is a pleasure in Jerusalem. When physical circumstances require it, buses and taxis are readily available and comparatively inexpensive.

°Recommended are *Carta's Jerusalem Guide* and *Carta's Jerusalem Map*, conveniently available in a single plastic binding.

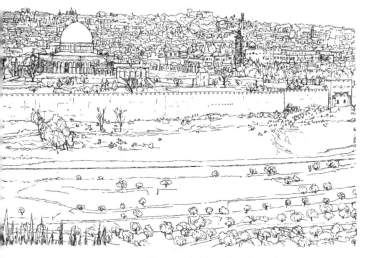

Panorama of Jerusalem from the Mount of Olives   11

JERUSALEM

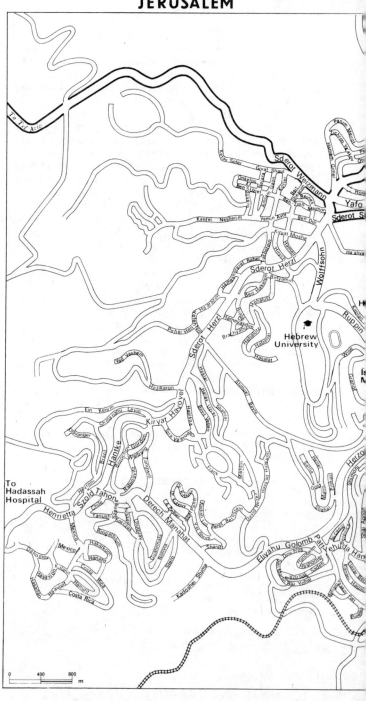

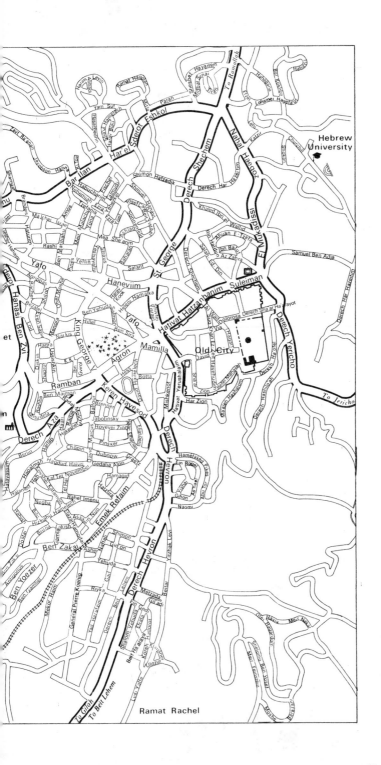

13

JERUSALEM: THE OLD CITY

The Old City under the lights, viewed at night from — for instance — the Yemin Moshe** sector, is a scene of spectacular beauty. Within it, in the daytime, the scenes range from bustling fruit and vegetable markets to venerable buildings which are charming and fascinating — and sometimes awe-inspiring. No short description can ever do justice to the sites and shrines, but a few must be mentioned in each of the four quarters — Muslim, Christian, Armenian and Jewish. Since the populations have shifted across the generations, and will doubtless shift again with the reunification of the city, today's Muslim Quarter overlays what was once the Jewish sector (with historic synagogues ravaged, and now being restored); several important Christian churches are in the Muslim Quarter; a leading mosque is now in the Christian Quarter...

The Lithostratos

Muslim Quarter

Sisters of Sion Convent and Ecce Homo Church, with the best opportunity to view the Lithostratos (which, until recently, was believed to be the original surface of flagstones which covered the courtyard in Jesus' time).

St. Anne's Church, with a museum, considered one of the best extant examples of the Crusader churches, according to tradition the birthplace of Mary and the site of Jesus healing the paralysed man.

The Via Dolorosa*, with churches and chapels at the various stations.

Adjoining the Muslim Quarter: the Temple Mount, with the Dome of the Rock* and El Aksa* Mosque.

St. Anne's Church

Christian Quarter

Church of the Holy Sepulchre*.

Church of St. John the Baptist (11th cent., Greek Orthodox), with earlier Byzantine church foundations (5th cent.).

Greek Orthodox Patriarchate and Seminary, with library.

El Khanqa Mosque (Sufi Muslim), once the seat of the Crusader Patriarch of Jerusalem.

St. Saviour's Church and Convent, with library, headquarters of the Roman Catholic Franciscans in Eretz Israel.

Jaffa Gate

Armenian Quarter

Cathedral of St. James (Armenian), with Chapels of Sts. Etchmiadzin and Stephen.

Folklore Museum, situated in the "Old Yishuv" courtyard.

Gulbenkian Library.

Mardigian Museum.

Syrian Orthodox Church and Monastery of St. Mark (12th cent.).

Yohanan Ben Zakkai synagogue

Jewish Quarter

"The Four Synagogues:" Eliyahu Hanavi**, Istambuli, Rabban Yohanan Ben Zakkai**, K'hal-Zion.

The German church of St. Mary (12th cent.).

Habad Synagogue, a Hasidic centre.

Hurvat R. Yehuda Hehasid.

The "Nea" Church (to be opened in the near future).

Ramban** Synagogue.

The Western Wall* of the Temple Mount.

JERUSALEM: THE NEW CITY

The first settlement outside the walls (1860) was in the area now called Yemin Moshe**, for the sponsor of the move from the crowded quarters of the Old City. The windmill and museum now memorialize the benefactor: Sir Moses Montefiore**. Mea She'arim, the Orthodox Jewish sector, was begun in 1875. Hereafter are identified some of the sites and shrines which the pilgrim, given sufficient time in Jerusalem, may find rewarding to search out.

Montefiore's Windmill

Abyssinian Church and Monastery (Ethiopian).
Albright Institute of Oriental Research**.
Baba Tama Bucharan Synagogue, Bucharan quarter.
Biblical Zoo.
Chagall Windows* at the synagogue of Hadassah Medical Centre.
The Garden Tomb.
Hebrew Union College, King David Street.
Hebrew University, Givat Ram campus (National Library, Institute of Contemporary Jewry).
Hebrew University, Mount Scopus campus (Harry S. Truman** Peace Centre, Hillel Foundation and Jacques Lipchitz sculpture: "The Tree of Life" situated at Hadassah Hospital).
Heichal Shlomo, King George Street, with museum and library.
Italian Synagogue, Hillel Street.
Jewish Theological Seminary, Neveh Schechter.
Kennedy Memorial**.
Monastery of the Cross (11th cent., on 5th cent. ruins) (Greek Orthodox).

National Library, Hebrew Univ.

Mount Herzl, with museum and tomb of Theodor Herzl**.

Rockefeller Museum**.

Russian Church (Russian Orthodox), in the Russian Compound.

St. Andrew's Church (Church of Scotland).

St. George's Cathedral and Close (Anglican).

St. Stephen's Church (Roman Catholic Dominicans) and École Biblique.

Sanhedria Tombs.

Second Temple Period Jerusalem, model at the Holyland Hotel (see Herod's Jerusalem*).

Sheikh Jarrah** Mosque.

Shrine of the Book*.

Tomb of Simon the Just**.

"Tombs of the Kings," Nablus Road — actually tomb of Heleni Hamalka**.

Yad Vashem*.

Yeshurun Central Synagogue, King George Street.

Y.M.C.A., King David Street.

Russian Church

Jerusalem outside the walls of the Old City includes sites and shrines of beauty and venerability. The original City of David lies outside the present wall, erected by Sultan Suleiman** (1520–66), and so too the section along the south wall now called Mount Zion. In the Kidron Valley below David's City and on the opposite hillside to the east are some of the most sacred sites of all greater Jerusalem. Since 1967 they have been accessible to pilgrims of all faiths.

Mount Zion

American Institute of Holy Land Studies (f. 1958).

David's Tomb and the Cenacle*.

Diaspora Yeshiva (f. 1949).

Dormition Abbey (Roman Catholic Benedictines).

House of Caiaphas (Armenian Church; Matt. 26:63–64).

Martef HaSho'ah (Chamber of Martyrs of the Holocaust).

Mosque of the prophet David.

17

Kidron Valley

Absalom's Monument (actually dating from the 1st cent.).
Grotto of Gethsemane (Roman Catholic Franciscans).
Hezekiah's Tunnel*.
Mary's Tomb, revered by Muslims and Christians (Greek Orthodox, with Armenians, Syrian Jacobites, Copts, Abyssinians).
St. Peter Gallicante (Roman Catholic Assumptionists; Matt. 26:69–75).
St. Stephen's Church (Greek Orthodox).

Absalom's Monument

Gethsemane and Mount of Olives

Basilica of the Agony /"Church of All Nations" (Roman Catholic Franciscans; Matt. 26:36).
Church of St. Mary Magdalene (Russian Orthodox).
Dome of the Ascension (a mosque since the 12th cent.).
Dominus Flevit Church (Roman Catholic Franciscans; Lk. 19:41–44), with important ruins and tombs.
Pater Noster Church (Roman Catholic Carmelites).
Russian Orthodox compound: churches, monastery and tower.
Tomb of the Prophetess Hulda, with Grotto of St. Pelagia (d. 457).
"Tombs of the Prophets" (traditionally Haggai, Malachi, Zechariah).

Dominus Flevit Church

JERUSALEM: THE SURROUNDING COUNTRYSIDE

Not only is Jerusalem itself full of sites and shrines worth visiting: at a short distance in any direction are churches and synagogues and mosques, excavations and ruins of historic note.

Abu Ghosh (W.): the place where the Ark rested until David** brought it to Jerusalem (I Sam. 7:1–2), with a monastery of the Ark of the Covenant (Roman Catholic: Sisters of St. Joseph of the Apparition); the ruins of a Crusader church built by the Knights Hospitaller (12th cent.); and the ruins of a Byzantine church built over an old synagogue (with mosaic floor). Col. David Marcus** was killed here in the War of Independence.

Abu Ghosh

Beitin, just north of Ramallah: the Biblical Bethel, where Jacob wrestled with the angel and received his blessing, and was named "Israel" (Gen. 32:24–32).

Beit Shemesh, west by south: with the nearby tel, important evidences of Canaanite and Philistine settlements; here Samson courted Delilah (Judg. 16:4). Beit Shemesh, like Beit Guvrin a bit further south, has impressive natural caves.

Bethany (E.): a village often visited by Jesus (the story of Mary and Martha, Lk. 10:38–42, and the raising of Lazarus, John 11:43–44), with Tomb of Lazarus — a shrine since the 4th century and a Muslim mosque; Church of St. Lazarus (Roman Catholic Franciscans); a Greek Orthodox church; and the ruins of a Benedictine monastery which the Crusaders rebuilt into a church.

Ein Kerem (S.W.): birthplace of John the Baptist (Lk. 1:68), with a Church of St. John (Roman Catholic Franciscans), with grotto; a Church of St. John (Russian Orthodox); a Church of the Visitation (Roman Catholic Franciscan).

19

Bethany

Emmaus: perhaps the most important Christian location (Mk. 16:12, Lk. 24:13ff) still in dispute. Early church fathers placed it near Latrun; was it El Kubeiba (N.W.)?

Latrun (W.): a strategic point in many wars — including the revolt of the Maccabees, Bar Kokhba's revolt, the Crusader battles, the British campaign (1917), and the wars of 1948 and 1967. The setting is the Aijalon Valley, where in battle with the Canaanites Joshua called upon the sun to stand still (Josh. 10:12–13). There are two beautiful monasteries, both Roman Catholic: the Cistercian Abbey and — next to ruins of "The Church of the Maccabees" (3rd cent. Byzantine) — the Silesian monastery. At the former a 3-faith community called "Neveh Shalom" is being developed.

Mizpa (N.): where the prophet Samuel appointed Saul to be king (I Sam. 10:17–27), with excavations.

Motza (W.): the first modern agricultural settlement in Eretz Israel (1894).

Nabi Samwil (N.): supposed tomb of the prophet Samuel (I Sam. 25:1), with a mosque over the crypt, built inside a Crusader church.

Nabi Samwil

AKKO

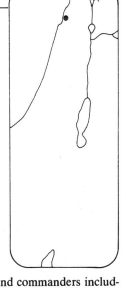

An ancient port, Akko (Acre) has been a setting for decisive historical moments across millennia. Controlling the great land route from the Bosphorus to the Nile, controlling a major trade route from Mesopotamia to the Mediterranean, it has been a valued fortress for Phoenicians, Assyrians, Persians, Crusaders, Saracens, Turks and British. Alexander the Great's successors named it "Ptolemais" and St. Paul knew it as such (Acts 21:7).

Captured by the Crusaders (1104), lost, and recaptured in 1191 in one of the mightiest military actions in the history of the Near East — with armies from Denmark, the Netherlands, England, Swabia, and commanders including the Archbishop of Canterbury and Richard the Lionheart, it remained under Crusader control until their final withdrawal (1291). The Mongols and the Mamelukes, who captured and laid waste so many great cities, never took Akko. Akko was the major port of entry for Christian warriors and pilgrims during the Crusader kingdoms, defended by a line of outlying fortresses which included Yehi'am* (Judin).

AKKO (ACRE)

During the siege of 1191 there was founded the military order of the Teutonic Knights, who, when the Holy Land was lost, acquired their chief fame as conquerors of the Baltic area.

St. Francis of Assisi landed at Akko (1219) on his way to proclaim Christian truth to the sultan, who listened politely and let him go. Teobaldo Visconti was in Akko on pilgrimage when news reached him of his election to the papacy (Gregory X: 1271–76). He is chiefly remembered for convoking the Council of Lyon (1274), which effected a temporary reunion of the Greek and Latin churches.

Napoleon Bonaparte, after conquering Egypt and Jerusalem, was stopped at Akko (1799) in his drive toward the east. Napoleon's plan to sever the lifelines of the British Empire, which had only recently (1763) defeated France for control of India and North America, was thwarted at Akko under command of Ahmad Pasha al-Jazzar ("the Butcher"). The beautiful al-Jazzar Mosque (built 1781–82) contains his sarcophagus.

The Citadel, a Turkish fort built on 13th century Crusader foundations, is well worth viewing. In the crypt of St. John of Acre, underground, the enormous stones of Crusader fortifications can be seen. Within the Citadel, captured Jewish freedom fighters were confined during the last years of the Mandate authority; a Museum of Courage memorializes those who died there. Portraits of Jews executed by the British hang in the corridor leading to the death chamber.

At a short distance to the north, off the main road, lies the shrine with exquisite gardens of the founder of the Baha'i faith (see Baha'i Shrines*). A few kilometres further north are Lohamei Hageta'ot* and Nes Amim*.

Al-Jazzar Mosque

MOSQUE OF
EL AKSA

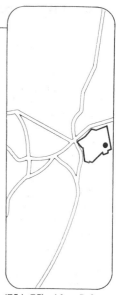

Sharing the Temple Mount with the golden-domed Dome of the Rock*, the silver-domed Mosque of El Aksa is one of the three most sacred shrines of Islam. Known as "the further mosque," it has prayer niches in the direction of Medina and Mecca.

The present mosque is largely the product of a renovation carried out in 1938–42, directed by the Egyptian Department of Monuments, under the British Mandate authority, but the original mosque was built by Caliph Abd al-Malik al-Walid** in 715. Before put to secular use by the Crusaders, the mosque was three times destroyed by earthquakes and rebuilt by Caliph (754–75) Abu Jafar Abdullah al-Mansur, Caliph (775–85) al-Mahdi and Caliph adh-Dhahir (in 1034–36). After Saladin (see Salah ad-Din**) conquered Jerusalem from the Crusaders (1187), reconstruction was undertaken. A grave incident occurred on 21 August 1969, when the mosque was set on fire by a deranged Australian. The pulpit of inlaid ivory, a structure of great beauty, was destroyed. Renovations are proceeding.

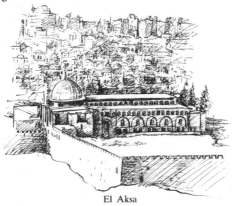

El Aksa

East of the mosque are the legendary "Solomon's Stables." The Crusader kings of Jerusalem and the Knights Templar (f. 1118 under Baldwin I) used the vaults for their horses.

Nearby, in the Jewish Quarter, the Emperor Justinian built a great church, consecrated in 543 as the New Church of Mary Theotokos ("Nea" Church), which remained in use for some decades after the first Muslim conquest. Materials from this building were used in later construction on the Temple Mount.

23

BASILICA OF
THE ANNUNCIATION

Nazareth, a town not mentioned in the Scriptures he knew, and viewed rather contemptuously by his contemporaries — "Can any good come out of Nazareth?" (John 1:46) — was the place of Jesus' birth and youth. Today there are many churches, monasteries, and other religious institutions in the city, maintained and staffed by the major Christian denominations.

One of the most beautiful edifices in Christendom is the Basilica of the Annunciation, built with extraordinary aesthetic taste and devotion by the Roman Catholic Franciscan Friars, 1955–65. The site, one of those identified by St. Helena**, mother of the Emperor Constantine, is revered as the place where the angel Gabriel appeared to Mary and told her of her son (Lk. 1:26–38).

Before the present construction, the Franciscans carried out careful archaeological excavations, and the present basilica of modern design incorporates in a highly imaginative way the sacred grotto, portions of the Byzantine church

NAZARETH

(c. 427), and the Crusader church erected by Tancred ("Prince of Galilee"). Little remains of the earliest church-synagogue, in which Jewish Christians — possibly governed by a caliphate of Jesus' own family — once worshipped.

The Annunciation Church is decorated by many stunning art forms, including mosaics and stained-glass windows from Ethiopia, Mexico, Japan and other far-flung Christian communities; mosaic panels celebrating the 1964 visit of Pope Paul VI**; wall paintings and mosaics portraying Mary as perceived by Christians in many lands. The basilica, although decoration is still proceeding, is one of the finest representations of the historical depth and ecumenical breadth of Latin Christianity.

Basilica of the Annunciation

In the city are many churches of note, including the Church of St. Joseph (also Roman Catholic Franciscan), and the Greek Orthodox Church near Mary's Well.

A short distance north of Nazareth is Kafr Kana (Cana), scene of Jesus' first miracle (John 2:3–9). Ruins here include evidence of an early synagogue-church.

A short way to the east is Mount Tabor. In 1924 the Roman Catholic Franciscans built there a beautiful sanctuary of the Transfiguration (Lk. 9:28–36).

North of Mount Tabor is Kafr Kama, one of the few Circassian villages in Israel. (Another is Rihaniya, north of Safad*). The Circassians are Muslims who came a century ago to escape persecution in Tsarist Russia. They enjoy their Israel citizenship and have served with distinction in the Israel army and border patrols.

Northwest are the ruins of Tzippori, one of the places of refuge for the Sanhedrin after the destruction of the Temple (70 C.E.); one of its leaders at that time was R. Yehuda Hanasi**. Excavations have exposed a synagogue mosaic (3rd cent.), a Byzantine church and Crusader basilica. The Crusaders set forth from Tzippori to their great defeat at the Horns of Hattin (1287). North of Tzippori are the ruins of Yodfat, where thousands of Jewish patriots perished in battle against the Romans in the Zealot revolt; their commander — Josephus Flavius — went over to the Romans (67 C.E.) and lived to write his histories.

Near Nazareth, to the southwest, is the first farming *moshav* in Eretz Israel: Nahalal (f. 1920).

THE BAHA'I SHRINES

For sheer beauty, few buildings in the world can compare with those erected at the international headquarters of the Baha'i faith in Haifa. On the slopes of Mount Carmel, overlooking the blue Mediterranean, the shrine of the forerunner of the movement (the Báb, martyred in Persia in 1850) attracts attention by exquisite lines and beautiful colour. On the grounds nearby are the Archives building and the Seat of the Universal House of Justice, both of stunning classical lines in white marble.

A few kilometres away, just north of Acre, is the shrine of the founder, Bahá'u'lláh. In a nearby building he spent his last years in house arrest, a prisoner of the Ottoman Empire ("Holy Muslim Empire").

Both shrines are surrounded by large expanses of incomparable gardens, lovingly tended. The variety of trees, bushes, flowers and birds remind the visitor of the Garden of Eden which lies in the human past — and to which a perfected humanity shall one day return.

Baha'i Shrine, Haifa

Shrine of Bahá'u'lláh

The forerunner of the Baha'i faith, the Báb ("the Gate"), issued his original call on 23 May 1844. Arising out of Shi'ite Islam, his message of a coming age of peace and justice and universal brotherhood of all peoples soon won a multitude of adherents — some 20,000 of whom shared his martyrdom at the hands of a vengeful establishment. He had announced that he would be followed by a greater manifestation, and that role was in 1863 assumed by Bahá'u'lláh ("the Glory of God"), who is recognized as the founder of the faith. Bahá'u'lláh (1817–92) taught that there are in human history successive revelations of one evolving truth. The great teachers of spiritual truth are honoured, and a core of universal truth is recognized in the teachings of the great living religions. This truth comprises a sacred law which is the foundation of society and civilization.

Bahá'u'lláh's successor was 'Abdúl-Bahá ("the Interpreter of the Faith"), who travelled in America and Europe. Adherence had by then spread beyond Persia and the Middle East. 'Abdúl-Bahá (d. 1921) was in turn succeeded by Shoghi Effendi ("the Guardian of the Faith"), upon whose death in 1957 the supervision of the work was assumed by a Council of nine members.

Today there are c. 100,000 Baha'i congregations, with adherents in 170 independent countries and many dependencies. Strategically located temples have been erected around the world, symbols of a religion whose essential message carries promise of the coming unity of all mankind. Locations include Wilmette (Illinois), Sydney (Australia), Kampala (Uganda), Panama City and the Taunus hills (near Frankfurt, Germany). A new temple is being built in Samoa, and another in India.

BANIAS

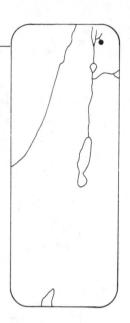

At its headwaters the Jordan, reckoned a holy river by many, has four main sources. Of these the Banias pools, fed underground by the lake Birket Ram, are especially interesting. Before an earthquake a century ago, the underground river issued directly from a cave — as impressive for the volume and beauty of its flow as, for example, the giant spring which pours into the Missouri River near Great Falls, Montana, or the Blautopf from which emerges the river near Ulm (Germany). Today the water near "the Cave of Pan" seeps out of the porous rock and detritus and is gathered in pools popular with bathers and photographers.

Baal and Pan were worshipped at Banias in early times. Caesarea Philippi was built here by Herod's son, Philip, after the division of Herod's kingdom among his three surviving sons, and was prominent in early Christian history (cf. Matt. 16:13–18). The city was destroyed in 1157 by Syrian Muslim forces in a struggle with the Crusaders.

Banias

To the north towers Mount Hermon (2,224 metres), a snow-capped ski area. To the south the crystal clear river flows toward Lake Kinneret* (the Sea of Galilee). The Jordan River is the lifeline of the area, just as the great lake — from which the national irrigation system draws water for the arid territory southward — is the centre of major truck farms, carp pools and diversified small industry. Before the irrigation system was developed to its present level, however, the damage done by centuries of absentee landlords and misuse of resources had to be repaired. Today dozens of fish ponds and gardens now flourish where not long ago large stretches of malarial swamps dominated the river basin.

Banias is situated at the foot of the Golan Heights, and the pilgrim should take the road up the steep eastern side of the Great Rift. From near the top his spirit will respond to the pictorial beauty of the settlements and cultivated fields along the river. And in a reflective moment, even if not a military expert, he will understand clearly the terrible danger those ridges and their gun displacements posed to the farmer families below when they were earlier in hostile hands.

Sources of the Jordan. Near Tel Dan we find a fountain flowing up out of the earth, and the water flows down to join the waters from Banias. Nearby is Ussishkin House**, a nature study institute. Two other sources of the Jordan also derive from the mountains of southern Lebanon. Near Metulla, a small town founded in 1896 and later placed under the patronage of Baron de Rothschild**, a beautiful waterfall (Hatanur) marks the entrance of the Ayun River into Israel. Nahal Senir enters Israel at Rhajar.

Majdal Shams: a Druse village on the southern slope of Mount Hermon. Among other Druse settlements are Beit Jann and Rama near Mt. Ha'ari, after Mt. Hermon and Mt. Meiron the highest mountain in the country, Bi'na near Karmiel and Mas'ada near Birket Ram. The Druse are a Muslim denomination dating from the 10th century, numerous in Palestine from the early 17th century. Their religious and communal order are closed to outsiders. Persecuted by the Muslim establishment elsewhere, they have fought valiantly in Israel's wars of survival; they have their own family courts and also representatives in the Knesset.

Kfar Gil'adi: a kibbutz (f. 1916) near Kiriyat Shmona, with a striking monument to Josef Trumpeldor** and comrades, who fell in 1920 defending the settlement of Tel Hai against marauders. The kibbutz served as a base for the smuggling of "illegal" Jewish immigrants (before the founding of the State), across the borders with Syria and Lebanon.

Mivtzar Nimrod: ruins of a Crusader castle off the road between Banias and Majdal Shams, the road once heavily travelled between Damascus and Akko. It is named after the Biblical mighty hunter Nimrod (Gen. 10:8–9). During the Crusader and Mameluke periods, the castle was called Kal'at es-Subeiba, according to Christian and Muslim sources.

Dan: the northernmost town in Biblical times — "Dan to Beer-sheva" (I Sam. 3:20). One of the "high places" which the prophets condemned, it was the place where Jeroboam set up a golden calf to lure the people from the Jerusalem shrine (I Kings 12:25–30, Amos 8:14). Excavations have revealed ruins dating back to the 2nd millennium B.C.E.

BEER SHEVA

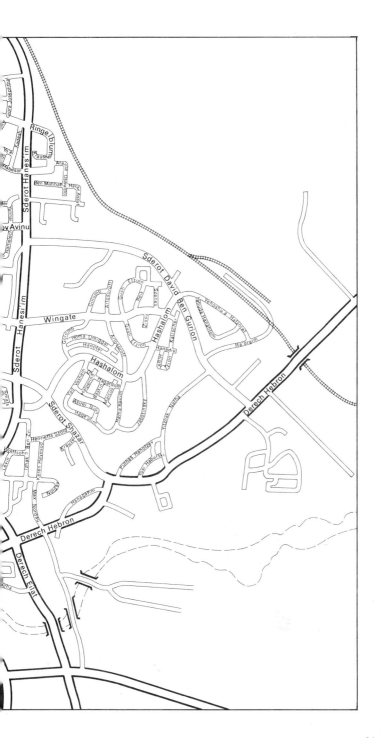

31

BEER SHEVA

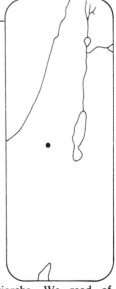

Beer Sheva, for centuries a sleepy town on the edge of the desert, is today the modern capital of the Negev. New industries, fine crops from fields irrigated by Israel's national water system, a fine young university (Ben-Gurion University of the Negev), and an influx of new settlers have combined to make an exciting city where a few years ago the most interesting activity was the camel market.

Archaeological digs in Beer Sheva and its environs have revealed ancient walls of mud and stone, and even more ancient caves once used for human habitation. The earliest Biblical stories associate Beer Sheva with the patriarchs. We read of Abraham's covenant with Abimelech (Gen. 21:25–34), his well (21:30) and grove (21:33); of Isaac's well (26:32–33); and of how Joseph's father and brothers set out for Egypt (46:1ff) from this place. Of the physical marks of these events nothing remains, except perhaps the well: the permanent marks are imbedded in the memories of the peoples of the three major monotheistic religions who call themselves children of Abraham.

Optically, Beer Sheva is chiefly interesting today for its university, with several buildings of imaginative design and functionality.

The University's Institute for Desert Research is located at Sde Boker*, to the south into the Negev.

Abraham's Well, Beer Sheva

BEIT ALFA

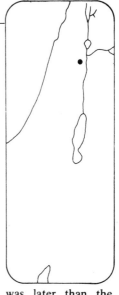

In 1928, during digging at the kibbutz just west of Beit Shean*, a mosaic was discovered which when completely excavated revealed one of the most beautiful ancient synagogue floors in the Holy Land. A magnificent mosaic portrays the scene of Abraham and Isaac before the altar, with a ram caught in the thicket (Gen. 22:1–13). Another panel depicts the signs of the zodiac, while a third panel shows Jewish religious emblems such as a *shofar*, lamp, *menorah*. There are also four faces which appear at first to be human, but on inspection they are allegorical — portraying the four seasons. Built in the 6th century, the Beit Alfa synagogue was later than the building of Galilean-type synagogues, such as the one at Bar'am, a splendid relic northwest of Safad*.

Mosaic panel, Beit Alfa

Nearby is the Sakhne (Gan Hashelosha), a natural marvel and place of popular resort. A beautiful clear underground river — like that of Banias* — emerges from the foot of the mountain to provide several giant pools for bathers.

To the west, halfway to the modern town of Afula (f. 1925), is Gid'ona, where Gideon camped and chose 300 of the most astute warriors to fight the Midianites (Judg. 7:5–22).

To the south is Mount Gilbo'a, where the Philistines slew King Saul with his sons (I Sam. 31:1–6), the mountain which King David cursed during his lamentations for the king and his friend Jonathan (II Sam. 1:17–27).

33

BEIT HATFUTZOT
(DIASPORA MUSEUM)

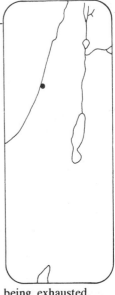

A priority visit for the pilgrim, the Diaspora Museum on the campus of Tel-Aviv University portrays 2,500 years of Jewish history. Originally proposed in 1959 by the World Jewish Congress as a way of bringing about creative discourse between Israeli and Diaspora youth, its present form was conceived (1970) by Abba Kovner (b. 1918), resistance fighter, poet and storyteller. (See also Nahum Goldman**.) Joining aesthetic sensibilities and modern technics in a marvelous way, the Beit Hatfutzot began its service to public education 15 May 1978. It can be visited many times without its intellectual and emotional impact on the viewer being exhausted.

The most diverse techniques are used to provide the visitor with a review of the highpoints of Jewish life and death. Audio-visuals, slide-shows and mini-movies, video booths and computer print-outs supply information at levels exciting to school children and informative for teachers and research specialists. By common consent of several hundred thousand public visitors, as well as museum professionals, the Beit Hatfutzot is one of the outstanding museums of the world.

At risk, two features are here singled out from the three floors of exhibits. One is the set of large and exquisitely constructed models of synagogue buildings from different periods — a building from the Spanish period, showing Arabic influence; the Renaissance synagogue at Florence, with a dome of Byzantine style; a building from Japan, in pagoda form; a wooden synagogue of Russian Poland; a stunning modern building (Beth Shalom, Philadelphia). The other is the set of computer booths where the inquirer can type in the name of a stetl or ghetto destroyed by the Nazis and receive a print-out of the history of that portion of a civilization that is gone.

Model of synagogue from Worms, Germany (destroyed 1938)

BEIT SHEAN

Beit Shean is one of the oldest cities in Israel. Archaeological excavations have revealed many strata of human settlement. Among the later ruins are a splendid Roman amphitheatre, considered the best preserved in Eretz Israel, and a Samaritan synagogue. Artifacts from the tel reveal its importance as a Philistine city, an Egyptian city, and a Roman city (when, as Scythopolis, it was the leading city of the "Decapolis," League of Ten Cities).

Bible students remember Beit Shean for the shattering defeat of King Saul at nearby Mount Gilbo'a and the subsequent display of his body, and the bodies of his sons, on the Philistine city walls (I Sam. 31:8). By Solomon's time it had been subdued and turned into headquarters for an administrative district.

Among its noteworthy inhabitants was Estori HaParhi**, Jewish topographer of Eretz Israel in the 14th century.

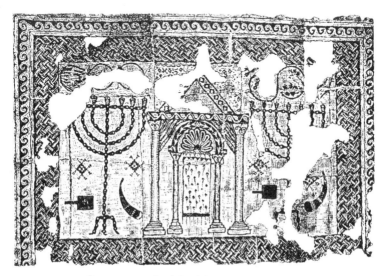

Synagogue mosaic of the Ark of the Law, 6th cent.

BEIT SHEAN

Just west of Beit Shean is Beit Alfa*.

South in the Jordan Valley but a few kilometres is a set of religious *kibbutzim*: Ein Hanatziv**, Tirat Tzevi (see R. Kalischer**), Shluhot and Sde Eliahu (see R. Gutmacher**).

A short run to the north is the beautiful view of the Jordan Valley from the impressive ruins of the Crusader castle Belvoir (see Yehi'am*).

Roman theatre, Beit Shean

BEIT SHE'ARIM

Between the Carmel range and Nazareth, Beit She'arim is noted today for the large necropolis in which were buried some of the most famous figures in Jewish history. The burial place consists of caves cut into the rock; the largest of the catacombs contains c. 400 tombs. Inscriptions show that the bodies of communal leaders were brought from Beirut, Antioch, Mesopotamia, Arabia and Yemen.

The reputation of the city, which flourished from the time of the Bar Kokhba revolt (132–35 C.E.) until it was destroyed during a 4th century revolt, was based upon its role as a seat of the Sanhedrin. R. Yehuda Hanasi** was buried here, and also his two sons R. Simeon and R. Gamaliel.

Near the catacombs are a reconstructed synagogue (2nd cent.) and a museum, and a monument to A. Zeid**.

On the heights to the south is the Carmelite Monastery of St. Elijah (see Haifa*).

A short distance northeast are the settlements Alonei Abba, Beit Lehem Haglilit and Neveh Ya'ar, founded by the Tempelgesellschaft, a Pietist sect which came from Wuerttemberg to prepare in the Holy Land for the advent of the Messiah. The "German Colonies" in Haifa, Jerusalem and Jaffa had the same origin, a century ago (1868).

Lion sarcophagus, found at Beit She'arim

CAESAREA

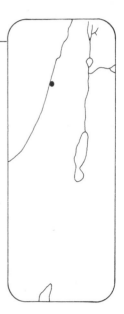

Caesarea was the capital of Herod the Great (see Herod's Jerusalem*), which he named for his patron Caesar Augustus and built into a massive display of Hellenistic culture. The splendid ruins of an aqueduct, hippodrome, theatre, forum, residences and public buildings may be seen. A recent find carries an inscription with the name of Pontius Pilate.

Peter baptized Cornelius, the first gentile convert, in Caesarea (Acts 10:24–48). Paul was imprisoned in the city for two years (see Acts 25 and 26 for the trial and defence) and, having appealed to Caesar as a Roman citizen, was shipped from there to Rome.

The hostility between the pagans and the Jews was strong, and a massacre of c. 20,000 Jews in 66 C.E. launched the countrywide Jewish revolt which ended with

Inscription of Pontius Pilate, found at Caesarea

"Israel Liberated" coin

defeat and the destruction of the Temple (70 C.E.). Caesarea also served as a major base and supply base during the Bar Kokhba revolt, and among the captives brought to the city and martyred by the Roman occupation was R. Akiva**. In spite of persecution and the prevailing paganism, a Jewish community continued which numbered some distinguished Talmudists. There are remains of an early synagogue (4th–7th cent.). It was also a strong Christian centre under the pagan emperors: the church father Origen (185?–254?) moved there from Alexandria and established an academy of learning.

After the accession of the Christian Emperor Constantine, and his establishment of control over the whole Roman Empire (in 324), Caesarea became an important episcopal see. Eusebius "of Caesarea" (260?–340?), church historian and ecclesiastical advisor to the emperor, was an episcopal delegate to the Council of Nicaea (325).Under the Crusades it was again a major Christian centre and was the port where Frederick II (Holy Roman Emperor: 1215–50), a leader in the 5th Crusade, and Louis IX ("Saint") of France (King: 1226–70), a leader in the 6th Crusade, landed. The city was devastated by the Muslim forces in 1265, completely destroyed in 1291, and regained significance only in the present century.

The Romans celebrated their victory over the Jewish insurgents by minting at Caesarea a coin engraved "Judaea Capta." With independence (1948), the State of Israel cast a coin engraved *Yisrael Hameshuhreret* ("Israel Liberated").

Near Caesarea is kibbutz Sdot Yam (f. 1940), from which Hannah Szenes** went to her fateful mission and heroic death.

To the north is Ramat Hanadiv, a fine public park and tomb memorializing Baron Benjamin Edmond de Rothschild**, "Father of the Yishuv," and his wife Ada.

On the coast, a short distance north on the arterial highway, is kibbutz Ma'agan Michael**, with the memorial Beit Gail**.

CAPERNAUM

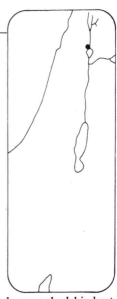

Kfar Nahum (Capernaum) on the Sea of Galilee (see Lake Kinneret*) was the main centre of Jesus' work and teaching. Many parables and miracles are recorded of his activities in or near the city. Here he made his second home, after Nazareth (Matt. 4:13–16) "his own city" (9:1). Along the shore he recruited Simon Peter and his brother Andrew (4:18–20). Peter's House and a neighbouring synagogue and school (4th–5th cent.) have been excavated by Roman Catholic Franciscan Friars (1969ff). In the city Jesus cured the servant of the centurion who had built the synagogue of that time (Lk. 1:1–10). Up the hill to the west he preached his best known sermon (Matt. 5–7). On the opposite shore, probably near a place today called Al Kursi, he healed the man possessed, the evil spirits passed into a herd of swine and the natives urged him to go home (Matt. 8:28–34). Down the lake but a short distance is Tabgha, the place where he fed the multitudes (Matt. 14:15–21). To the northeast but a short distance is Korazim, condemned by Jesus (Matt. 11:21) in a set of imprecations which also included Capernaum (11:23).

Excavations have exposed the ruins of an old synagogue (3rd cent.), with mosaics. It seems clear that in Capernaum, as in Nazareth, there was a synagogue-church, used by Judaeo-Christians. An octagonal church (5th–6th cent.), built on the site of Peter's House, has also been discovered, with a splendid mosaic floor.

The Tabernacle as represented in the synagogue at Capernaum

A circuit of the Golan Heights may be undertaken from Capernaum, running by Kuneitra to Mount Hermon, then down past the headwaters of the Jordan (see Banias*) to Safad*. Certainly no one can understand the courage of the early settlers, or for that matter of any of the farmers until 1967, who has not looked out over the valley from the former Syrian artillery displacements.

On the way a stop at Gamla is recommended, where excavations have revealed some of the most impressively situated fortifications used by the Jewish patriots against the Roman occupation armies, set on the heights amidst natural beauties of unforgettable splendour.

CHAGALL WINDOWS

In the synagogue at the Hadassah-Hebrew University Medical Centre on the western outskirts of Jerusalem are found the famous stained-glass windows done by Marc Chagall (b. 1887) to commemorate the Twelve Tribes of Israel.

Chagall left his native Russia in 1923 and made his home in Paris — with periods spent from time to time in Israel and the USA. His work in stained glass is found also in other prominent places, such as the UN Secretariat in New York, Metz Cathedral, and his paintings and other art forms are also world famous. Mosaics and tapestries by Chagall grace the Knesset building in Jerusalem. (Some of his early works, confiscated by the Soviets and suppressed during a half-century of "Soviet realism," were shown in the Pushkin Museum in 1979.)

The windows surrounding the upper level of the synagogue, three to a side, depict the twelve tribes in vivid colour. Each window is devoted to one of the sons, and the artist portrays the father's blessings — "Reuben... unstable as water" (Gen. 49:4); "Judah is a lion's whelp..." (49:9); "Gad... shall overcome at the last" (49:19)... From the texts in Genesis 49 and the blessing of the tribes (Deut. 33) Chagall chose the rich colours and figures appropriate to the personalities of Jacob's sons.

There are two bullet holes which remind the viewer of the battles of the young country for survival. First installed in 1962, the windows had to be restored after the Six-Day War. The story is that Chagall was cabled for instructions and replied, "You take care of the war and I will take care of the windows." They did, and he did.

Hadassah, the Jewish women's movement with about one-third of a million members in the USA, was founded in 1912 by Henrietta Szold**. The movement supports extensive educational, medical and other work in Israel.

In the plaza of the Hadassah Hospital on Mount Scopus may be found a striking statuary by another renowned artist, Jacques Lipchitz (1891–1973): "The Tree of Life." Lipchitz left the casts of his works to the Israel Museum, Jerusalem, where they are on display.

Reuben

Gad

(By courtesy of Ministry of Communications, Philatelic Services)

CHAY BAR

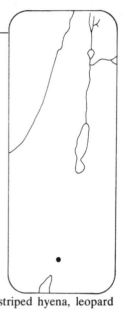

Near kibbutz Yotvata (f. 1957) north of Eilat, the beautiful resort town on the gulf which joins the Red Sea, is the Biblical Wildlife Reserve. Beginning in 1964 and opened to the public in 1977, a voluntary work was launched to gather animals of all species that were known in the land in Biblical times — especially those in danger of extinction.

Roaming over some 3,237 hectares (8,000 acres) of semi-desert, the animals include such rare species as the Somali Wild Ass, the Asiatic Wild Ass (Jer. 2:24), the Sahara Oryx, the Ibex, the Addax, the Negev Gazelle — along with the ostrich (Lam. 4:3), desert lynx, striped hyena, leopard and other beasts less rare.

The Biblical Zoo, in north Jerusalem, has also collected birds, animals and reptiles mentioned in the Bible — and is accessible to visitors who cannot undertake the trip to the large open reserve in the south.

In the area which was once Lake Hula, north of Lake Kinneret*, but now drained and largely under cultivation, a section has been set aside for a natural reserve with flowers, bushes, plants and grass now or once native to Eretz Israel.

Eilat, with five guest hotels, is a paradise for swimmers and scuba divers, as are *moshav* Nevi'ot (80 kilometres further south) and *moshav* Di Zahav (145 kilometres further south), both founded in 1971. Eilat is the centre of jewelry made from the semi-precious Eilat stone, shading from light green to deep turquoise. Eilat's community centre is named for Philip Murray** (1886–1952), American labour leader.

Just north of Eilat are the striking rock formations known as Amram's Pillars and Solomon's Pillars. Timna, near the latter, is the earliest copper mine ever worked (c. 4000 B.C.E.), popularly but erroneously called "Solomon's Mines." Solomon's copper works were at Ezion-geber, on the shore east of Eilat.

Ostriches

DAVID'S TOMB
AND THE CENACLE

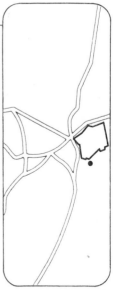

A single complex of buildings on Mount Zion houses three shrines of religious note, sites identified with three distinct periods of history. And two of them are important to three religions. The shrines are "the Tomb of David," "the Room of the Last Supper" and Martef HaSho'ah (memorial to the martyrs of Bergen-Belsen and other camps). Yet no shrines in the Holy Land more fully reflect the tangled web of history, sectarian and fratricidal feuds, property conflicts and dubious diplomacy than the building which today houses "David's Tomb" and "the Supper Room." The identifications are precarious. For that matter, "Mount Zion" itself has been a shifting location as Jerusalem has gone through millennia of earthquakes and wars, of building, destruction and rebuilding.

From outside, the land is "Zion." Within the land, Jerusalem is "Zion." And within the Holy City, "Zion" refers properly to the Temple Mount. But because of the construction a millennium ago of two Muslim shrines (El Aksa* and Dome of the Rock*), Israel authorities have not taken over control and use of the Temple Mount. The centre of pilgrimage for the Jewish devout has remained the Western Wall*.

With the Jordanian conquest of East Jerusalem, 1948–67, Jews were not allowed (contrary to the armistice agreement) to approach the Western Wall. During that period tens of thousands turned to "the Tomb of David" as the next most holy shrine. But when was David's burial place first located there, rather than by the Pool of Siloam or — for that matter — in Bethlehem (where St. Jerome and his contemporaries placed it)? The lower section of the building, now identified with David's Tomb, may have been in the early centuries the tomb of St. Stephen, the first Christian martyr (Acts 7:57–8:2). The identification with King David became widespread at the time of R. Benjamin of Tudela (see Mitudela**). Subsequently the site passed back and forth between Muslim and Roman Catholic and Jewish authorities, being a source of diplomatic and local intrigue for centuries. At present the building is surmounted by a mosque's minaret.

The Cenacle is associated with one of the central events of Jesus' ministry, the Lord's Supper (Lk. 22:7–20, I Cor. 11:24–26), which has been recollected and reenacted innumerable times in various forms and places since the original. Documents locating the room of the Last Supper in the neighbourhood go back to the 2nd century. Many edifices

43

David's Tomb

Last Supper Room

have been constructed, destroyed and rebuilt, as wars and revolutions and internecine Christian strife have shuttled a room so designated between different religions and denominations. The Israel authorities resolved the conflict between Roman Catholic Franciscans and the Muslims (who had in 1524 turned the present room into a mosque) a few years ago by declaring it an historic site open to the public but closed to organised religious use.

David's Tomb and the Cenacle are worth visiting to see where in recent centuries pilgrims of three faiths have honoured the memories of two of the Holy City's greatest sons — and to reflect upon the dangers inherent in religious devotion undisciplined by charity.

Martef HaSho'ah was founded in 1949 by survivors, to commemorate the memory of the 6,000,000 Jewish victims of the Nazi "final solution to the Jewish problem." The cavernous setting is appropriate. The lighted candles bespeak the tribute of those who know that "to have faith is to remember." The individual plaques which recall lost towns, ghettoes and families will leave no sensitive person unmoved.

Nearby is the Diaspora Yeshiva (f. 1949), a unique Orthodox Jewish school for training young Jews of all backgrounds — and some gentile students as well — in the Torah. There is a World Peace Centre, which aims to cultivate amity among the faith communities represented on Mount Zion, and a Chay Biblical Garden where the flora of the Bible are collected and tended.

One of the outstanding institutions on the Mount is the American Institute of Holy Land Studies, founded and led 1958–78 by Dr. G. Douglas Young, where thousands of Christian college and seminary students and teachers have studied Jewish language and history in the City of David and the land of the fathers.

The most impressive unit on the Mount is the Dormition Abbey of the Roman Catholic Benedictines of Beuron (Ger.). The building was begun in 1900. The octagon form stands in architectural succession to Christian buildings at Aachen, Ravenna and Constantinople.

The Armenian Church of St. Saviour, along with the House of Caiaphas, completes the picture of major religious institutions on the Mount. The Armenians were the first Christianized nation (301 C.E.), and in spite of severe repression and persecution — including the slaughter of over half of their people in the last decades of "the Holy Muslim Empire," 1894–1915 — have kept their loyalties throughout the centuries.

DOME OF THE ROCK

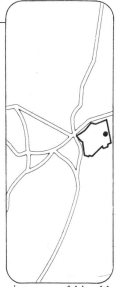

Of all the many beautiful buildings in Jerusalem, it is safe to say that the Dome of the Rock is the best known. Standing alone in the cleared space of the Temple Mount, it focuses attention. Paintings and photographs of the skyline feature it. One of the most exquisite edifices in the world, in this sector of the globe only the Baha'i Shrine* on the slopes of Mt. Carmel can compare with it for sheer beauty.

In terms of antiquity, the site is beyond comparison anywhere, for according to religious lore it is built over the cave which houses "the foundation stone of the universe." Here Abraham offered to God the precious son of his old age, Isaac, the heir through whom the promises he had received of God were to be fulfilled. And here, perceiving his faithfulness, the angel provided a ram as a substitute, conferred a blessing and renewed the promises (Gen. 22:1–18). Here Solomon built the First Temple, which his father — a man of war — could not build (I Kings 6:1–8: 21), and invoked the Lord's blessing upon the house and the people (I Kings 8:22–53). Here Zerubbabel built the Second Temple, when King Cyrus permitted the First Return from Exile (538–515 B.C.E.), which with renovations stood until the destruction (70 C.E.) and profanation (c. 130 C.E.).

Following the Muslim conquest, Caliph Abd al-Malik, the Umayyad, (646?–705) built the shrine (687–91) to offset the centering of attention on Mecca and Medina. His son and successor built El Aksa*. According to a tale that was circulated at that time, the prophet Muhammed made a heavenly night flight from the rock on his horse "El Burak," and visitors are still shown the hoofprint in the cave below the shrine.

The Crusaders built extensively on the Mount, but spared the Dome of the Rock. After the Muslim re-conquest of Jerusalem (1187), Jews were barred from the Mount but allowed from time to time to pray at the Western Wall*. During the Jordanian conquest of East Jerusalem (1948–67), Jews were barred from the Wall. After the recapture of the Temple Mount on 7 June 1967, however, the Israel government has respected the Muslim shrines of Dome of the Rock and El Aksa ("the further mosque"), both in use for more than a millennium.

Dome of the Rock

EIN GEDI

Between Kh. Kumran (Qumran) and Masada*, on the western shore of the Dead Sea, is a large oasis often mentioned in documents of early Jewish history: Ein Gedi. There is a lovely waterfall approached by a short walk. Longer paths lead to the ruins of an Israelite fort, a Roman fort, an ancient synagogue with a mosaic floor (discovered in 1970), a Chalcolithic temple dating back to c. 3000 B.C.E. Nearby, today, is a kibbutz with a guest hotel.

Near Ein Gedi is the cave where, according to tradition, David spared the life of King Saul, who came to slay him (I Sam. 24). In the famous love song, the suitor praises his beloved by evoking the sensuous atmosphere of the oasis (Song of Songs 1:14). (When was the book "spiritualized" to represent the love of God for his people or the love of Christ for his church, respectively?) Ein Gedi was also an outpost during the Zealot revolt of 66–70 and the Bar Kokhba revolt of 132–35.

A nature reserve contains diverse desert and water plants and trees, as well as such animals as the ibex, hyrax (rock badger), fox, wolf, hyena and leopard.

> The Dead Sea is the lowest surface on earth (398 metres below sea level), and the scattered oases along its western bank but serve to accent its impressive denial of life. In the Scriptures it is a place of destruction and death — of the rain of brimstone and fire upon Sodom and Gemorrah (Gen. 19:24) and the death of Lot's wife (v. 26). Conversely, when the prophet is shown a vision of the restoration of the earth to its full beauty, nothing could be more dramatic for him than the healing of the waters and the return of flourishing life to a cleansed salt sea and its shores (Ezek. 47:8–12).

HAIFA

Haifa is a beautiful modern city, looking out over the Mediterranean. The view from the top of the tower building of the University of Haifa, especially as the lights come on in the evening, is stunning. The Technion, Israel's university of technology, is less picturesquely situated, but world-renowned. The chief religious sites are the Baha'i Shrines* and the scenes associated with the prophet Elijah**.

Near the shore, in the city sector Bat Galim, is the Cave of Elijah — venerated by Jews, Christians and Muslims. On the mount occurred the dramatic showdown between him and the idol-worshippers sponsored by Queen Jezebel (I Kings 18:20–40). On the site is the Monastery of St. Elijah (f. 1827; Roman Catholic Carmelites). Elijah's challenge still rings across the centuries: "How long will you go limping between two opinions? If the Lord be God, follow him: but if Baal, then follow him!"

Mount Carmel continued to be a gathering place for hermits and monks and was in the early centuries of the Common Era a centre of Palestinian monasticism. In the Crusader period the Order of Carmelites was founded (1207). In 1291 and again in 1799 communities of monastics were slaughtered by the Muslims, but they returned to build the monastery and are there today.

Monastery of
St. Elijah, Haifa

Near the monastery is one of the major Druse settlements, Daliyat-el-Carmel (see Nebi Shueib*). Below it to the east, in the northern reach of the Valley of Jezreel, is Beit She'arim*.

In Haifa's Museum of Ancient Art are found exhibits of artifacts from Canaanite burial caves (14th–13th cent. B.C.E.).

Modern historic sites include the houses of Laurence Oliphant** and his sometime secretary Naftali Imber**. There are also buildings of the "German Colony," from settlements c. 1868 by a German Pietist sect led by Christopher Hofmann (1815–85).

Across the bay is Akko*, and but a short run down the coast are the ruins of Atlit, the only unconquered Crusader fortification (see Yehi'am*).

47

HAIFA

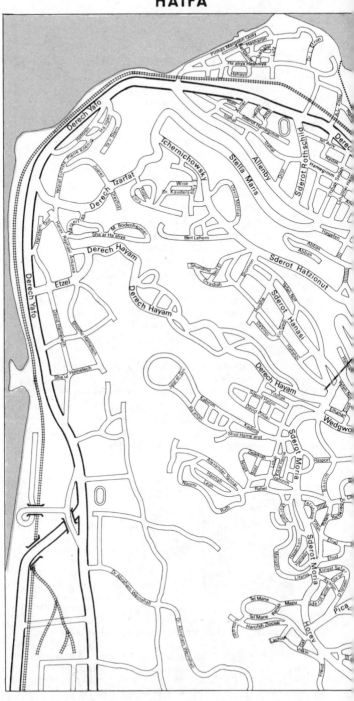

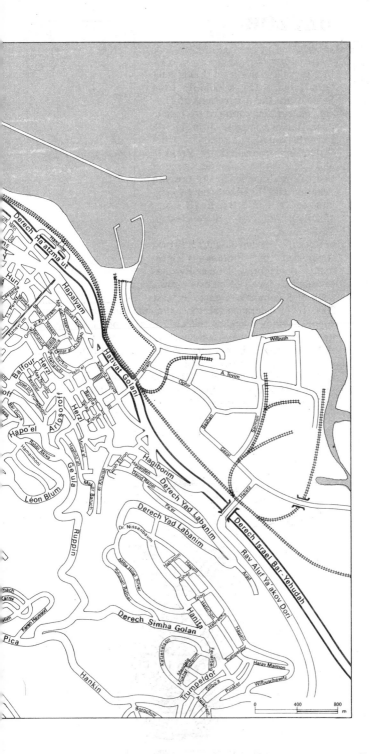

HATZOR

In the valley north of Lake Kin-neret*, but a few kilometres from Safad*, are the excavations of Hat-zor. Hatzor was captured by Joshua in the initial conquest (Josh. 11:10). Its army, under Sisera, was de-feated by forces led by Barak** and Deborah**. Solomon made it one of his strategic cavalry posts (a "chariot city"). Destroyed by Tig-lath-pileser in 732 B.C.E. (II Kings 15:29), it was first rediscovered in 1875.

Recent archaeological work, supervised by Professor Yigael Yadin of Hebrew University, has revealed 22 levels of cities — going back of Solomon's reign to at least 2000 B.C.E. Perhaps the most dramatic find was the water supply system. Digging revealed that rather than depend upon outside springs (see Hezekiah's Tunnel* and Megid-do*), the city engineers sunk (c. 850 B.C.E.) a deep shaft to draw from underground supplies.

At the kibbutz Ayelet Hashahar nearby (f. 1916) the visitor may enjoy a display of some of the finds — along with excellent hospitality.

Ivory cosmetic spoon found in Hatzor

50

HEBRON

Hebron is one of the four holy cities of Eretz Israel, associated especially with King David. It was the centre of Absalom's revolt against his father (II Sam. 15:7ff). In recent decades it has achieved notoriety as a centre of Arab extremism and terrorist activity. In 1929 a Muslim mob, aroused by demagogues, fell upon the ancient Jewish community and murdered 59; in May of 1980 a company of young people, including many Americans, returning from Sabbath services were attacked — with 7 fatalities and many injured.

Hebron was David's capital for 7 years before, with the death of Saul and his sons, the elders came and invited him to become king of Israel as well as Judah (II Sam. 2–4). A tomb opposite Machpela Cave is assigned by tradition to Avner Ben Ner**, commander of the army of King Saul.

Machpela Cave, Tomb of the Patriarchs (and Matriarchs), is the most important shrine in the area — revered by Jews, Christians and Muslims. Pilgrimages to it became frequent from the latter part of the 7th century. Here Abraham, when Sarah died on the way from Bethel (Beitin) to Beer Sheva*, purchased the cave (Gen. 23:1–20) which became the burial place for her — and later for Abraham, Isaac, Rebecca, Leah and Jacob (Gen. 25:8; 49:29–32, II Sam. 2:1). Rachel was buried near Bethlehem (see Kever Rahel**).

The large building over the site was built under Herod the Great, with additions of minarets and a mosque many centuries later. The mosque was originally a Byzantine church and was converted by Baybars, the Mameluke ruler

Machpela Cave, Hebron

51

of Egypt. Until the last century access was difficult even for non-Muslims of high diplomatic rank in Christendom, and Jews were barred. Since 1967, under Israel supervision, access has been guaranteed to pilgrims of all faiths concerned.

A beautiful mosque in Hebron, Sheikh Ali Bakta, dates from the Mameluke period (13th cent.).

At a short distance is "Abraham's Oak," a great tree by which stands a Russian Orthodox monastery. This is the location (Mamre) tradition has assigned to Abraham's reception of the angels who told him of the child to come to Sarah and him in their old age (Gen. 18:1–15).

There are interesting archaeological sites to the south: Tel Zif, Khirbet al-Karmil (see I Sam. 25:2–42 for the story of Abigail), Samua.

HEBRON

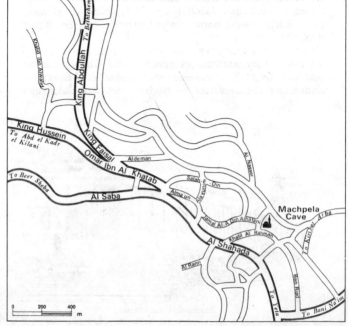

HERODION

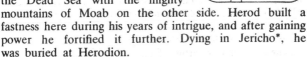

Herod the Great (King of Judea: 37–4 B.C.E.) was one of the great builders of history. Among the many sites worthy of a visitor's attention which still display his power and pride after nearly two millennia are Caesarea*, the Machpela Cave at Hebron*, the Western Wall*, Masada*, and Herodion. (See also Jerusalem*.)

Herodion, in the hills south of Bethlehem, is spectacularly situated at the top of a volcano-shaped mountain. The view from the top affords a panorama toward Bethlehem and Jerusalem to the west, and to the east the great valley of the Dead Sea with the mighty mountains of Moab on the other side. Herod built a fastness here during his years of intrigue, and after gaining power he fortified it further. Dying in Jericho*, he was buried at Herodion.

Excavations have identified a synagogue and ritual bath, and a Byzantine chapel added centuries later. Herodion was a fortress of Jewish patriots in the Zealots' revolt (66–70 C.E.), and again from 132 to 134 during the days of Bar Kokhba.

Herodion

The road going east from Bethlehem divides, the right fork leading over a good road to Herodion, the left fork providing a long and difficult road to one of the gems of ancient Palestinian monasticism: the *laura* ("narrow way") of Mar Saba (f. 483). St. Saba (439–532) founded four *lauras* and six monasteries and was for a time supervisor of all the monastic colonies in the Judean Hills. His body, taken during the Crusades to Venice, was returned to Mar Saba following the Ecumenical Council: Vatican II (1965).

Women are not allowed within the monastery (Greek Orthodox Church, Basilian order), but there is a "women's tower" outside. The setting in the lower Kidron Valley has a wild beauty which makes the excursion worthwhile, with a patient and careful driver. At one time several hundred monks lived in the caves around the great stone building. Many of them were slaughtered by the Persians in the invasion of 614. Within the monastery is a cave and a chapel memorializing St. John of Damascus (700?–754?), the last of the great Greek church fathers, who died there. (See Karantal*.)

HEROD'S JERUSALEM

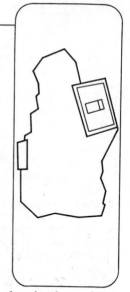

Herod I (73?–4 B.C.E.) was one of the great tyrants of history. His claim to legitimacy was based upon his marriage to Mariamne, niece of the last of the Hasmonean rulers. His claim to power was based upon a grant from the Roman emperor which declared him King of Judea — a title to which he gave substance by three years of successful war, ending in the capture of Jerusalem, the massacre of male rivals to the throne, the destruction of the power of the Sanhedrin. Later he murdered Mariamne and several of his sons. Of Herod the Christians tell the story of the slaughter of the innocents (Matt. 2:13–16), evoking the memory of the slaughter of the firstborn by an earlier tyrant, Pharaoh.

Herod brought the Roman province of Judea into the Hellenistic cultural orbit. This and the ruthlessness and luxury of his lifestyle were deeply resented by devout Jews. However, his building mania, skillful diplomacy and favour in Rome brought economic and political prosperity to his domain.

At Herodion* and Masada* he built fortresses. He built Sebaste, near Shechem*, the old capital of the northern kingdom. He made Caesarea*, which he made a great Roman city and named for his patron, his own capital. In Jerusalem he rebuilt the Temple (see Western Wall*) and ordered other great public works.

Modern archaeologists have enjoyed many celebrations thanks to Herod "the Great." One of the most fascinating projects was supervised by Professor Michael Avi–Yonah (1904–74) of Hebrew University: the construction of a large model of Jerusalem at the time of Herod, located on the grounds of the Holyland Hotel. Here Jewish and Christian pilgrims can see, executed in fine detail, how the Holy City looked at the time of the Second Temple's restoration; how it was known to Jesus, Peter and Paul; how it was seen by R. Hillel** and Gamaliel the Elder**, before the destruction.

Second Temple model, Holyland Hotel

HEZEKIAH'S TUNNEL

One of the most remarkable engineering feats in history was accomplished with the most elementary tools: pick and muscle. That feat was the hewing of a tunnel 530 metres through rock, and nearly 45 metres down, to secure Jerusalem's water supply against an impending siege. More remarkable yet, the channel was cut from both ends and the crews met underground — with but the slightest displacement in the walls of the completed tunnel.

Report of the accomplishment was engraved in ancient Hebrew script upon the wall near the outlet. After the rediscovery of the water tunnel in 1880, the inscription was cut away and lodged in the Oriental Museum, Istanbul. (Eretz Israel was then a province of the Ottoman Empire.) There is a good deal of winding in the course of the tunnel, perhaps because the work crews followed natural seams in the rock. The excitement of the moment when the teams met so precisely still resounds from the ancient inscription. This is how it was cut through: in the midst of their hewing with picks, with yet three cubits to go, the voice of one was heard calling to his partner, for there was a crack in the rock to the right and another to the left. At the time they finished the cutting, the stone cutters met pick to pick, face to face. And the water flowed from the spring to the pool.

Inscription found inside Hezekiah's tunnel

The compilers of the records of the ancient kings were as impressed as we are today (I Kings 1:45, II Kings 20:20, II Chron. 32:30).

King Hezekiah's plan was executed c. 702 B.C.E., as the forces of the Assyrian king Sennacherib were approaching the city. The spring was thereby hidden from view at the top of the watercourse. At the outlet, 20 metres lower, the water was gathered into a large partially hewn pool ("the Pool of Siloam") readily accessible to defenders of the City of David. Today's pilgrim can, if he wishes, traverse the whole length of the tunnel.

The Pool of Siloam later became a shrine to Christians because of a healing miracle of Jesus reported in John's Gospel (9:1-9). A church was built there in early times. Destroyed by the Persians in 614 C.E., its ruins were discovered in 1896.

55

CHURCH OF THE HOLY SEPULCHRE

When the mother of Constantine the Great (sole Roman emperor from 324 to 337) St. Helena, made her pilgrimage to the Holy Land (c. 325) to mark the sites identified with the life and work of Jesus, the location of the place of the crucifixion was established with greater certainty than most. For the Emperor Hadrian, in making Jerusalem a heathen city (Aelia Capitolina) by expelling all Jews and profaning the sacred sites of the Christians, erected a statue of Aphrodite at Golgotha and the tomb. Constantine was able to have the Roman construction and rubble cleared away and build a huge basilica enclosing both the place of the cross and the tomb donated by Joseph of Arimathea. (See Via Dolorosa*.)

Constantine's church was destroyed by the Persians (614), in the invasion that brought ruin to Christian centres throughout Palestine and death to so many thousands of monks and other Christians. Restored, destroyed again by the Muslim Caliph al-Hakim (1009), the church received most of its present form from the Crusaders.

After generations of unsavoury altercations between the Greek and Latin churches over control of the building, the political authorities decreed an arrangement which has provided use of certain facilities at certain hours to the Roman Catholics, Greek Orthodox and Armenian Orthodox, and to the Syrian Jacobites, Ethiopian and Egyptian Copts. This arrangement (the so-called *Status Quo*), decreed by the Ottoman Turks in 1752, has been maintained by subsequent governments. Under this decree sectarian disputes and riots have been reduced. But the problem of repairs and maintenance awaits the renewing work of a true ecumenical spirit among the Christians.

In the southwest quarter of the Old City, the Church of the Holy Sepulchre in its present form includes also the Chapel of the Resurrection, the Chapel of the Cross, the Chapel of Calvary, and a "Chapel of Adam" below. Within it are also designated the last five stations of the cross.

Since the middle of the 18th century there have been occasional sceptics who have argued against the traditional sites and located "the place of the skull" (Golgotha) and the tomb elsewhere. The main alternative site is the Garden Tomb, ninety metres up Nablus Road from the Damascus Gate. This view was given wide circulation by General Charles G. Gordon (1833–85), suppressor of the Teiping Rebellion in China and of the slave trade in the Nile Valley, who fell when Khartoum was besieged and captured in the Revolt of the Mahdi. (On Gordon's views see his *Reflections in Palestine*, 1884.)

JAFFA
AND TEL AVIV

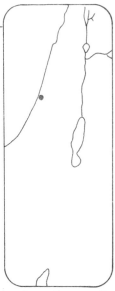

Jaffa was the ancient port through which came material from Hiram of Tyre to assist Solomon in building the Temple (II Chron. 2:16). (See Western Wall*.) Before that it had been a key port of the Phoenicians (the people of the sea, the "Philistines" of the Bible). It was the port from which the prophet Jonah embarked (Jonah 1:1–3). In early Christian teaching it was remembered as the place where St. Peter had his dream about clean and unclean foods (Acts 10:10–16), which he reported with significant impact in the church at Jerusalem (11:3–10). Through Jaffa came the occupation troops and supplies that besieged Masada*, after Vespasian slew the port's Jewish inhabitants. It was the chief port through which in the Middle Ages, before the Crusader kingdoms, Jewish and Christian pilgrims from Europe passed on their way to Jerusalem.

But these events, so important to religious history, left few visible signs and no distinct religious sites. The Monastery of St. Peter and Church of St. Anthony (both under management of the Roman Catholic Franciscan Friars) and the remains of the Sarona Colony (f. 1868) of the German Templer Society, like the flourishing modern industrial port, belong to another age.

Tel Aviv (f. 1909 and merged with Jaffa in 1949) is a thoroughly modern city, jointly with its suburbs containing more than 40% of Israel's population. Its major institutions include the Tel Kasila Museum, Tel-Aviv University, and Bar-Ilan University**. The latter is chartered by the Regents of the State of New York. At the Beit Hatanach, a museum of Biblical documents, the State of Israel came into being (14 May 1948). Beit Hatfutzot*, the Diaspora Museum, must be visited.

To the south, along the coast, lie the cities of the Philistines: Ashdod, Ashkelon and Gaza. On the way south the traveller passes Yavneh, the seat of the Sanhedrin under R. Ben Zakkai** and R. Tarfon**, and the place where the

Clock tower in Jaffa

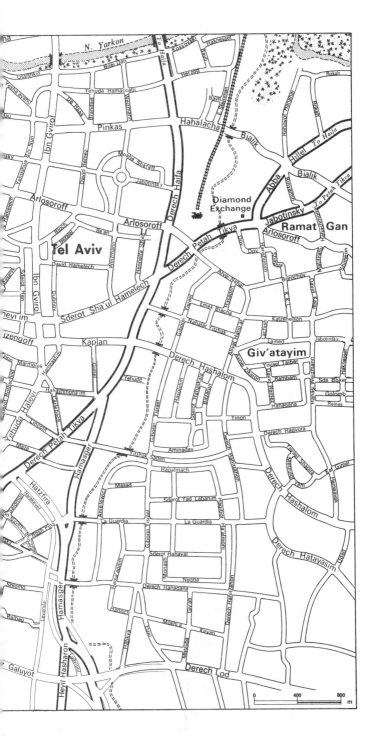

sages finalized the condemnation of the Judaeo-Christian sect (80 C.E.).

Ashdod was the city to which the Philistines brought the Ark of the Covenant, which they had captured from the Israelites (I Sam. 4:11), which brought disaster upon them and their allies in Gath and Ekron before they returned it with a peace–offering at Beit Shemesh (I Sam. 5:1–7:26). Modern Ashdod was founded in 1956.

Ashkelon was the traditional city of Herod's birth, which he enlarged greatly during his building mania. The Crusaders also built great installations there — and carried away a word which became common usage in the kitchens of their homelands: *shallot*, scallion. The modern city was founded in 1953.

Just south of Ashkelon is kibbutz Yad Mordechai**, its monument to the leader of the Warsaw Ghetto uprising and Holocaust Museum well worth visiting.

Gaza was the principal city of "the people of the sea," who came c. 1170 B.C.E. in flight from the Dorian invasion of the Greek islands. Here the blinded Samson, betrayed into the hands of his enemies by Delilah, consummated his battles by slaying more in his death than he had in his lifetime (Judg. 16:21–30). Nearby, according to Christian tradition, the Holy Family stopped on the return from Egypt. To the south is an excavated synagogue (early 6th cent.), with mosaics. The outstanding shrines in the city proper are the Great Mosque of Jamia al-Kabir, built with remains of a Crusader church, and the Mosque of Hashem (uncle of Muhammed).

To the northeast of Tel Aviv is a city, Petah Tikva, which has grown from the first agricultural settlement (f. 1878, renewed by Bilu pioneers in 1883).

Just outside Jaffa, to the southeast, is Mikveh Yisrael, the oldest agricultural school in Eretz Israel (f. 1870 by the Alliance Israelite Universelle).

At a further distance is Rehovot, site of the Weizmann Institute of Science** (f. 1934).

Just northeast of Rehovot is Ramla (f. 716), the only city founded by Arabs in Palestine. Notable shrines are the Great Mosque, formerly a Crusader cathedral; the White Mosque, built by Caliph Suleiman in 716, and the adjoining White Tower (completed in 1318). The Cisterns of St. Helena are an impressive piece of public works, built during the rule of Caliph Harun al-Rashid**.

Southeast of Ramla is Tel Gezer, one of the most famous archaeological excavations in the Holy Land, associated with the name of Nelson Glueck (1900–71), sometime president of Hebrew Union College. At one time a post for Solomon's cavalry (a "chariot city"), Gezer's strata go back c. 5,000 years. Noted are the 20 sacred pillars (stelae) which were unearthed at the "high place."

East of Jaffa–Tel Aviv is Lod, now known to the traveller for its airport but once renowned as a centre of Jewish and Christian activities. Lod was a centre of Jewish learning after the destruction of the Temple (70 C.E.). Later it was an episcopal see of the Christians, and in 415 the Synod of Lydda was held here — famous for the defence Pelagius (360?–420?) made of the freedom of the will against his theological adversaries, especially Bishop Augustine of Hippo (354–430).

JERICHO

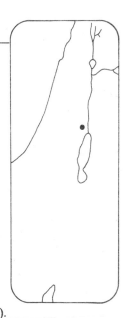

Jericho, "the oldest city in the world," lies in the Jordan Valley a short drive east from Jerusalem. Located near the entry of the river into the Dead Sea, the city is well below sea level. On the way down the traveller passes on the right two sites hallowed by tradition: by the road, "the Inn of the Good Samaritan" (Lk. 10:25–37); a short distance off the road, Nebi Musa Tomb, a Muslim shrine built (1290) by Baybars to memorialize the resting place of Moses (but see Deut. 34:7). To the left, approaching the valley, is a rough road which leads to one of the early monastic communities of the area (St. George of Coziba in Wadi Kilt; see Karantal*).

Jericho was the first settlement conquered by Joshua in Canaan (Josh. 6), in a dramatic action known to every school child. Modern excavations have verified the Biblical account, and have also exposed fortifications (Tel Jericho) dating c. 8,000 years before the Common Era.

The river is the site of a number of chapels commemorating the baptism of Jesus by John the Baptist (Matt. 3:16–17). Near the place called by the Arabs Kasr al-Yehud, where Joshua and his forces may have crossed the river, is a Greek Orthodox Church of St. John the Baptist, and near it a Coptic Monastery of the Holy Trinity (built 1933 by Empress Menen of Ethiopia).

Hisham's Palace, Jericho

In Jericho are the ruins (with mosaics) of the Na'aran synagogue (6th–7th cent.), and the splendid mosaics and ruins of Caliph Hisham's winter palace (8th cent.). A few years after its construction the palace was destroyed by an earthquake. Many of the art forms, excavated during the Mandate, are displayed at the Rockefeller Museum** in Jerusalem.

With all of the interesting sites and shrines, the trip down to Jericho is memorable above all for the view of the miracle of the life-giving river which runs from Banias* to the Dead Sea. On the other side rise the mountains of Moab, the giant ridge that runs far to the south and once provided a single spine for Asia Minor and Africa. From the heights Moses viewed the Promised Land (Deut. 34:1–4), and selected the young man who should lead the people in investing it (Deut. 31:7–8).

A short distance to the west is Karantal*.

Up the valley a few kilometres is Gilgal, in early generations the place where the kings were crowned (I Sam. 9:14).

A few kilometres to the south is Qumran, ruins where lived the Dead Sea sectarians who fled the world — and whom the world discovered in 1947 (see Shrine of the Book*).

JERICHO

KARANTAL

At a short distance from Jericho* is
the Monastery of the Temptation
(Lk. 4:1–13), set against a high
mountain such as that where Jesus
spent 40 days tempted by satan.
The original monastery was set on
the summit, and the Crusaders later
attempted to restore a church there.
Since 1895 the Greek Orthodox
Church has maintained and staffed
the present awesome edifice, nes-
tled into the high cliff, with a
splendid view of the Jordan Valley.

Karantal, more accessible to view
than Mar Saba or St. Catherine's
Monastery* in Sinai or St. George's
Monastery in Wadi Kilt, is rep-
resentative of a style of Christian life which once covered
Asia Minor and Egypt with communes. The authority of
those leading the life of retreat from the world was so great
in the church for some centuries that even emperors and
kings and churchmen of high position in the empire were
prone to defer to the monks. They had taken, and were
observing, the vows of poverty and celibacy. Men of affairs
like Jerome and Augustine and Ambrose deferred to the
monastic model, and wrote their own sets of rules and led
their own communities.

The monks dominated early synods and councils, and
their antipathy to women and to "the Jews" made itself felt
in a host of resolutions and decrees.

Monasticism was initially a protest movement. Early
monasticism reflected in part the temperament of the early
church, which was in tune with other Jewish sectarian
(anti–establishment) movements such as the Essenes (see
Shrine of the Book* on Qumran). When Christianity was
preferred and privileged by the Christian emperors, monasticism was a way for sensitive persons to escape from
accommodation and acculturation. In the Dark Ages, when
the empire fell apart into warring principalities — with
even the rulers little more than barbarous and illiterate
chieftains, the monastic communities preserved literacy,
liturgy, and obedience to a Law higher than that of the
jungle. Today the surviving centres in Eretz Israel are
maintained by little bands of Greek Orthodox monks, but
there are ruins of once great communes all over the Near
East.

The first monastic community in Palestine was established near Gaza by St. Hilarion (290?–371), who had been
a hermit in Egypt. Soon thereafter a *laura* ("narrow way")
was begun at Karantal. Most of the early colonies,
practicing the common life (cenobites), were surrounded by
numbers of hermits — living in caves outside the walls, but

St. George's Monastery in Wadi Kilt

subject in a general way to the supervision of the communal superior.

St. Saba (439–532) was one of the most gifted of the founders and superiors, and he began in 483 a community in the lower Kidron Valley which still bears his name. The monastery, destroyed in early medieval times, was repaired and rebuilt in the 19th century. Today, still intact, it is an impressive building set in a wilderness of extraordinary beauty (see Herodion*).

St. Theodosius (424–529) founded in 476 a large monastery east of Bethlehem. Like several others, it was then divided according to the nations of the members — with Greeks, Armenians and Slavs the major companies of recruits. The community was butchered and pillaged by the Persians (614), and again three times during the Muslim conquest of Palestine. Restored by the Crusaders, it again fell to Bedouin marauders and was restored by the Greek Orthodox in this century.

St. John of Coziba (440?–520?) was the founder of a monastery in Wadi Kilt, now approached by a bad road turning off the Jerusalem-Jericho highway near the sea level sign. St. George of Coziba (d. 620) was head of the community during its most flourishing era and its destruction in 614. The building, set in impressive and remote hill country, was restored at the turn of this century.

A significant insight into the scale of values then obtaining is gained by reflecting upon the fact that St. John of Coziba was elected Bishop of Caesarea, but served only a few months and resigned to return to the remote commune he had founded.

LAKE KINNERET

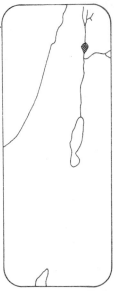

From the "Galilee man" of a half million years ago, whose remains were found in 1959 just south of the lake, to the modern pilgrim, Lake Kinneret has attracted and inspired farmers and poets and lovers of nature's wonders. The first kibbutz (Degania) was founded in 1910 at the outlet of the lake. Of it Rahel** wrote one of her best-known poems ("Kinneret"). The Jew moves instinctively from Jerusalem to Tiberias* on its shores, the Christian to Capernaum*.

The area is replete with synagogues and churches, both in ruins — for the destructions wrought by the Persians under Chosroes (614) and the Mamelukes under Baybars (Sultan: 1260–77) were as total as they could make them — and active. But the great source of wonder is the lake itself.

Through the national irrigation system the lake and the Jordan River, which feeds into it, supply the fertile farmlands of the immediate area — and also the half of the country which lies to the south, with 15% of the water and 85% of the population of Israel.

The "Sea of Galilee" was the centre of Jesus' ministry, the scene of such stories as the miraculous catch of fish (Lk. 5:3–11), the stilling of the tempest (Mk. 4:35–41), his walking on the water (Mk. 6:45–51). He recruited his first followers from fishermen.

Looking out over the lake from the west, from the "Mount of the Beatitudes," or from the east, from the ruins of the fortress at Gamla from which Jewish patriots fought the Roman invader, evokes the deepest feelings of recollection and wonder.

Church on Mount of the Beatitudes

Degania "A" is the burial place of such pioneers as A. Ruppin**, A.D. Gordon**, Otto Warburg**. At *kevutza* Kinneret nearby are buried B. Katznelson**, Rahel Bluwstein**, N. Syrkin**, Moshe Hess**.

Near the exit of the lake is Beit Yerah, where excavations have revealed many interesting relics, including a beautiful mosaic.

On the eastern shore and up into the Golan Heights, excavations at Afik, Eli Al, Ramot, Susita and elsewhere have revealed ancient synagogues and other evidence of early Jewish settlements.

LOHAMEI HAGETA'OT

Just off the coastal highway, a few kilometres north of Akko*, is the Kibbutz of the Ghetto Fighters, founded in 1945. As the name implies — ghetto fighters — the community was formed initially by survivors of the Holocaust.

Survivors are not a rarity in Israel, but few have done as much to insure that the teaching of that epochal event and its lessons shall be passed on to succeeding generations. The kibbutz has established a large archive and museum on the Holocaust, with valuable photographs, drawings and artifacts; an extermination camp model with precision of detail; a model of the Warsaw ghetto.

Translating the memories of this watershed event in the history of the Jewish people and of Christianity is a work which is expanding rapidly in several countries — notably in America, West Germany and Israel. Lohamei Hageta'ot's contribution — documentary, plastic and educational — is substantial, and should be viewed.

Neighbouring Lohamei Hageta'ot is the Christian *moshav* Nes Amim*, where volunteers from many nations are helping to build up the land. The work is an expression of Christian concern for the survival and vitality of the Jewish people.

A short distance to the east are the substantial remains of the Crusader forts Yehi'am* and Montfort.

Museum at Lohamei Hageta'ot

MASADA
(METZADA)

Towering far above the Dead Sea, a massive rock formation jutting out from the edge of the Judean Desert has come to be one of the most widely known symbols of the human dedication to freedom. The Dead Sea, a great body of water ten times as salty as the ocean and rich in phosphates, is 398 metres below sea level — the lowest place on the earth's surface. Masada, accessible by foot path or cable car from a good highway, stands 434 metres above (slightly less than 40 metres above sea level).

To the east, across the valley, rise the great mountains of Moab — part of the great ridge which extends for thousands of kilometres down into Africa, reminding us that Asia Minor and Africa once shared a single spine.

First fortified by the Maccabees, the mighty rock plateau is over five kilometres in circumference at the base, 610 metres in length and 197 metres in width at the top. Herod made it his fastness during the period of intrigue which preceded his accession to the throne. Masada became a landmark in human history during the Jewish rebellion against Rome (66–73 C.E.) of which Josephus was the noted narrator.

During the Great Revolt (66–70 C.E.) refugees from Jerusalem joined the Zealots holding the fortress, whose numbers increased after the destruction of the Temple in 70 C.E. Against the large army commanded by Flavius Silva they held out for more than two years under the leadership

Masada

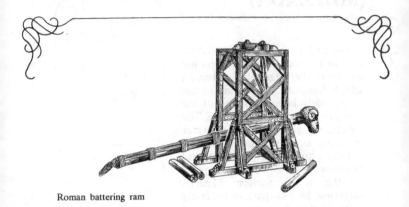

Roman battering ram

of Eliezer Ben Ya'ir. Silva, using thousands of slaves, raised an earthen rampart to bridge the chasm between the great abutment and the main plateau. Faced with certain capture or death in defeat, the defenders drew lots and gave themselves to ritual slaughter rather than yield to slavery.

Men and women, with their children, thus entered their final testimony against servitude to a foreign conqueror who had defiled their religious shrine and sought their submission. The Roman soldiers, entering the fortress on the morning after their *kiddush haShem* (honouring the Name), found some 960 bodies — and ample supplies of water, food and weaponry.

Excavation was initiated in 1963–65 by a team of archaeologists directed by Professor Yigael Yadin of Hebrew University, assisted by teams of international volunteers.

Masada is today the place where young recruits take their oath of loyalty and service in the armed forces of a restored Israel. The ceremony closes with the pledge: "Masada shall not fall again!"

Triumphal parade with Temple vessels — Arch of Titus, Rome

MEGIDDO

In the Jezreel Valley, a short distance southwest of Afula (f. 1925), is the ruin of an ancient city whose most dramatic time — according to some believers — lies before it: Megiddo, the Armageddon of the Christian book of Revelation (16:16).

Ancient Megiddo commanded the trade route between the civilization of the Nile Valley and the empires that rose and fell along the Tigris and Euphrates rivers.

Excavations in 1929–39, 1961 and 1969 have revealed 25 different strata reaching back 6,000 years. Buildings and walls, and artifacts displayed in the tel's museum, show how important the control post was to the Canaanites, the Hyksos, the Egyptians, the Philistines and the ancient Hebrews. It was assaulted by Joshua (Josh. 12:21); it supplied forces to Sisera, whom Barak** and Deborah** defeated and Jael slew (Judg. 5:19–27); it was used by Solomon as a "chariot city" (with Hatzor* and Gezer).

The museum at the tel displays a model of the ancient city, with a building from the time of King David. At the excavations, one of the most interesting sights is the water tunnel leading to an outside spring. Interesting too is the "Temple Precinct," where stood a series of temples to different gods.

When the Christian writer reported his vision of the apocalypse (Rev. 16:1ff), of the approaching final cataclysm, of the last battle between good and evil, he picked Megiddo for the confrontation — Megiddo, which had known colossal battles, sieges, fire and earthquake for millennia, was to be the epicentre. And he wrote of what he knew: sores, blood and blasting, scorching and drought, thunders and lightning and earthquakes, hail and famine. The atom bomb had not yet been invented.

Megiddo

CHURCH OF THE NATIVITY

The most terrible destruction to fall upon Christian sites and shrines across the centuries did not come from the pagan Romans or the Muslims: it came during the Persian invasion of 614. The established religion of the Sassanid Empire, which under Chosroes II (d. 628) conquered Syria, Palestine and Egypt and besieged Constantinople, was Zoroastrianism. Wherever they went the Persians pillaged and destroyed churches and monasteries, killing thousands of monks — with one exception: the Church of the Nativity in Bethlehem. According to tradition, the reason the Persian commander halted his forces at the entry was that over and around it were portrayed the Magi, the wise men from the east, wearing Persian dress. In the story of the nativity, the Magi had indeed their roles to play (Lk. 2:4–20).

The church, large and built like a fortress, stands over the substantial grotto which St. Helena identified as the stable back of the inn, in which Jesus was born. Within the grotto is one location with a star, said to mark the exact spot. In another location is the cave where St. Jerome (340?–420) lived for many years, while preparing the Vulgate version of the Bible and acting as spiritual director of a nunnery led by his patroness St. Paula of Rome (d. 404).

The ground floor of the basilica is impressive. At one point an opening has been made to expose to view a portion of the beautiful mosaic floor of the Byzantine period. The area before the altar and at either side is heavily decorated, especially by paraphernalia contributed earlier by the Russian Orthodox Church. Use of the sanctuary is shared by the Latins, Greeks and Armenians — all three of which also have monasteries for resident personnel.

The church which Constantine built was damaged during the Samaritan revolt of 529; Justinian rebuilt it. The Muslims respected the shrine during their conquest of the Holy Land. The Crusaders crowned their kings of

St. Jerome in Penitence, El Greco

Jerusalem there, and they also added substantially to the structure. After the re-conquest, in spite of the best efforts of Roman Catholic Franciscans and treaty agreements, there was open looting and deterioration. Sectarian strife among the several churches, earthquake (1834) and fire (1869) also did their worst. Today, under Israel's protection of shrines and historic sites and supervision of processions during Holy Days of the Christian calendar, comity agreements are maintained and pilgrims of all denominations have open access to one of Christianity's most sacred shrines.

BETHLEHEM

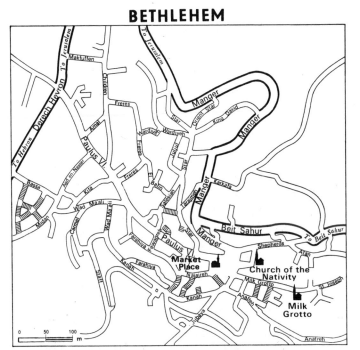

In Bethlehem itself are several minor shrines of venerability, including the so-called Milk Grotto and the House of St. Joseph.

To the east is Beit Sahur, with a field nearby which is associated with the Biblical story of Ruth. Here also are several different areas identified with the fields where the shepherds tended their flocks (Lk. 2:8–20); the one claimed by the Roman Catholic Franciscans is adorned by the beautiful chapel "Ad Pastores."

From Beit Sahur, the left junction leads to the Monastery of St. Theodosius and Mar Saba (see Karantal*), the right to Herodion*.

On the outskirts of Bethlehem is the Tomb of Rachel (see Kever Rahel**).

A short distance to the south are Solomon's Pools*.

Directly to the west is Beit Jalla, the location of many churches, monasteries and seminaries.

71

NEBI SHUEIB

A short distance west of Tiberias*, near the fateful battlefield where the collapse of Crusader power in the Holy Land was determined (Horns of Hattin, 1187), is one of the sacred shrines of the Druse communities. Nebi Shueib is dedicated to the memory of Jethro, father-in-law and advisor to Moses (Ex. 18:5–27), whom the Druse honour as a prophet.

The Druse, who number c. 40,000 in Israel, are in origin a branch of Islam. Although they participate fully as citizens, having their own family courts and members in the Knesset, having won a reputation as excellent soldiers and border guards, their internal community life is secret. No outsider knows Druse rites, rituals, or basic beliefs, except as they may be surmised from the facts of their history known to scholars.

Their founder, Muhammed Ibn Ismail al-Derazi (d. 1019), was a confidant of Caliph Abu Ali Mansur al-Hakim (985–1021), who tried to make Shi'ite Islam the established religion of Egypt. Al-Hakim is said to have declared himself an incarnation of the Deity, but this is a charge frequently made by their enemies against mystics who proclaim the indwelling of the Divine Spirit. Outsiders, we do not know the truth of it.

We do know that, savagely persecuted by orthodox Muslim governments, the Druse have built a good life in Israel.

> The Druse have, across nearly a millennium of generally precarious existence, become accustomed to building their settlements in mountainous, defensible locations. There is a considerable village, Majdal Shams, on the slopes of Mount Hermon, another — Daliyat–el–Carmel — on the ridge of Mount Carmel, another — Hurfeish — at Mount Zebul.

72

NES AMIM

One of the most important Christian centres in Israel is the *moshav* Nes Amim. Located in the western Galilee a few kilometres north of Akko*, and neighbour to the Ghetto Fighters' kibbutz (Lohamei Hageta'ot*), Nes Amim has gathered volunteers from many countries — Sweden, England, West Germany, Switzerland, the Netherlands, Canada and the USA.

The work of Nes Amim was begun by a remarkable medical doctor, Johan Pilon (d. 1975), who from 1950 had worked in the Scottish Hospital in Tiberias. In the years when the matter of the survival of the Jewish people came to the centre of theological discussion, he made in company with co-believers in the Dutch Reformed Church the spiritual pilgrimage from Hebrew Christian missions to Christian/Jewish dialogue and cooperation. They came to believe that after the Holocaust Christian credibility depended less upon verbalization and much more upon constructive fraternal work.

In 1960 the plan to establish a community of Christians who would help build up the Promised Land was confirmed

Nes Amim

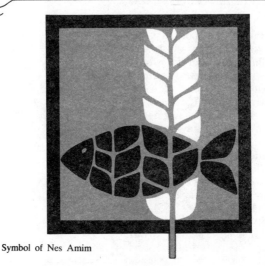

Symbol of Nes Amim

at an international conference in the Netherlands, and
initial approaches were made to the government of Israel
for accreditation. Land was purchased in 1962, and by 1964
some 25 volunteers were at work. In that year Shlomo
Bezek (d. 1971), a Dutch Jew, was seconded to Nes Amim
as a technical advisor by kibbutz Ayelet Hashahar. Thus in
the early years the spiritual and field work leadership of the
developing community was shared by two Dutchmen, a
Christian and a Jew, and their friendship symbolized the
relationship which Nes Amim purposed for adherents of
the two faiths in the Holy Land and in the Ecumene.

Nes Amim pioneered in building a flourishing rose
culture, which today ships daily to markets in western
Europe. Later an avocado plantation was started, and this
too has been very successful. In 1975 a conference centre
was built, largely with the assistance of German Protestant
churches. Here town meetings are held, and also Christian
and inter-faith conferences and seminars for residents of
Israel and conferees from abroad. Strong support has
continued to come from churches in the Netherlands, and
there are now Nes Amim "home boards" in Switzerland
and America as well as the Netherlands and the German
Federal Republic.

Magazine features and movie coverage have in recent
years featured this unique work of Christian/Jewish frater-
nity, including an American national TV educational
programme produced in "Bill Moyer's Journal."

Nes Amim ("Banner to the Nations," "Miracle of the
Nations") has reached the stage where it makes a genuine
contribution to Israel's agriculture and economy. It also
stands as a sign of what credible fraternal work may be
accomplished by Christians who have meditated on the
mystery of a restored Israel, who have mastered some of
74   the basic lessons of belief and action after the Holocaust.

SAFAD

On a majestic mountain northwest of Lake Kinneret*, Safad is one of the four holy cities of Eretz Israel — and the highest city in the land.

A naturally strategic post, it was a centre of the revolt against the Roman occupation in 66 C.E., and was later fought over by the Knights Templar, Saladin (see Salah ad-Din**) and Baybars. It is most famous, however, for the flowering of Kabbalistic learning which developed there with the influx of Jewish scholars driven out of Spain and Portugal (1492–96).

Among the luminaries of the Kabbalist period were R. Hayyim Vital**, R. Moshe Ben–Jacob Cordovero (1522–70), R. Solomon Alkabez**, R. Isaiah ha-Levi Horowitz, R. Josef Caro** and R. Isaac Luria (see Ha'ari**).

Numerous *yeshivot* and the first printing press in Eretz Israel (1578) helped to create a religious and literary renaissance in 16th century Safad. In the 18th century a series of natural disasters struck (earthquake, drought,

SAFAD

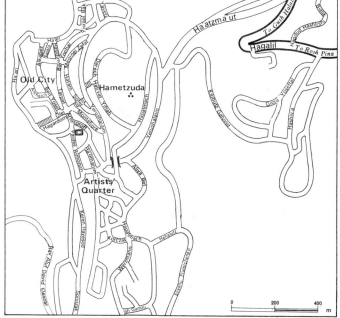

locusts), and in 1837 a massive earthquake killed thousands and virtually wiped out the community.

The present population is largely the result of recent settlement and growth, although several beautiful old synagogues — including the Ha'ari synagogue and the Caro synagogue — recall the splendour of another age.

Governor's House in Safad

Just to the east is Rosh Pina, the first Jewish village in the Galilee (1882).

A short distance to the west is Meiron, where large crowds each year make a joyful pilgrimage to celebrate Lag Ba'omer (33 days after Passover) at the tomb of R. Simeon Bar Yohai (see Shimon**). (The cave where R. Simeon and his son hid out from the Romans for 12 years is at Peki'in, near Ma'alot; Peki'in has a very old synagogue which may date back to his lifetime.) Near his tomb is the tomb of R. Yohanan Hasandlar**.

To the northwest is Bar'am, with two ancient synagogues excavated — one of them considered the best preserved example of early Common Era architecture.

North by east is Hatzor*.

Synagogue in Safad

ST. CATHERINE'S MONASTERY

Under terms of the Israel–Egyptian agreements, the western portion of the Sinai peninsula passed back to Egyptian control in January, 1980. Egypt had acquired control in 1910 and lost it in the attack and short war of 1967. The agreement provides, however, for continued access to St. Catherine's Monastery.

The remarkable church-fortress sits at the foot of Har Moshe ("Mount of Moses"; in Arabic "Jebel Mussa"), likely scene of one of the shaping events in human history (Ex. 20:1–17), sacred to Jews, Christians and Muslims. President Sadat of Egypt has said that he would like to have his burial place there. He has also proposed that chapels be built there by each of the faiths. Such shrines would signify a pledge of renewed efforts toward reconciliation and amity among the peoples of the three large monotheistic religions.

The monastery is reached by a short flight and/or by land travel. Named for St. Catherine of Alexandria (d. 307), it was built by Justinian (Emperor: 527–65) — who also built San Vitale in Ravenna and Santa Sophia in Constantinople. Of the genre of Mar Saba** and other great centres of early Christian monasticism (see Karantal*), it was once the centre of c. 6,000 hermits and cenobites. Today it is staffed by a handful of Basilian monks of the Greek Orthodox Church.

St. Catherine's itself is an institution of extraordinary beauty, with mosaics, gilded screens, candelabra and other decorations — including the oldest hand–painted icon in the world (6th cent.). In its valuable archives Constantin von Tischendorf discovered (1844) the famous *Codex Sinaiticus* (4th cent. Bible), and in 1950 a team discovered the *Codex Syriacus* and *Codex Arabicus* (4th–8th cent.). At a higher level, in the refectory are scrawled on the walls the names of some of the most redoubtable chieftains of the Crusader kingdoms. Whether the tradition that relates St. Helena to the place can be credited or not, there is a section of the complex that probably predates Justinian: "The Chapel of the Burning Bush" (Ex. 3:2).

Towering above the monastery, whose remoteness and fortifications so vividly signify the goals and dangers of monasticism in its heyday, is the Mount Sinai of tradition (2,712 metres). A favourite act of pilgrims, to be commended to the strong of heart and spirit, is an early hike to the top to greet the sunrise. There is a well-worn path, and the view out over the wild country traversed by Moses and the people escaping from slavery is one of earth's most inspiring prospects.

SDE BOKER

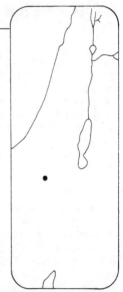

Sde Boker is a settlement south of Beer Sheva*, in the midst of an area which reminds an American of the Dakota badlands. Stark plateaus and deeply eroded canyons (*wadis*) bring distance and geological age into focus in a panorama of wild beauty.

The kibbutz was founded in 1952. Its best known member was a major architect of the State of Israel, David Ben-Gurion**. In the Research Institute and Archives nearby are being gathered the documents of the 67 years from his arrival in Eretz Israel (1906) until his death (1973). The facilities for visiting and resident scholars are being expanded steadily. Short-term leadership schools for young Israelis are held. Buses daily convey groups of older citizens to the pictorial exhibit and the tomb of Israel's "Founding Father."

Ben-Gurion was an advocate of the contributions of the deserts to human life, and several scientific projects of world significance are being carried on at Sde Boker — some with the university in Beer Sheva that carries his name. The projects cover hydrogeology, meteorology, climatology, desert architecture, energy conversion, desert botany, medicine for arid zones, nomad settlement, desert economics and environmental education.

David Ben-Gurion

One aspect of desert study involves attention to the civilization of the Nabateans, an Arab tribe who penetrated into Eretz Israel in the 1st century C.E. and created one of the most successful economies based upon skillful water retention and irrigation. At Avdat and Shivta, nearby, impressive ruins may be visited which tell of a society which for six hundred years (c. 4th cent. B.C.E.–2nd cent. C.E.) made the desert work and controlled the trade routes of those from the river civilizations of the Nile and the Tigris and Euphrates who wished to pass through.

SHECHEM

Today's Nablus (from Neapolis, the "new city" of Vespasian) is a volatile population, almost exclusively Muslim, with a record of terrorist activities. Nearby, at Tel Shechem and Sebastiya, are the ruins of several of the greatest cities of the ancient world. And nearby, on Mt. Gerizim, is the shrine of the Samaritans, a people that was once a major power in the Near East — until it destroyed itself by war, conducted with religious zeal, terrorism, and self-destructive revolts against both Jews and Christians.

Excavations at Tel Shechem have exposed strata of settlements reaching back to earlier periods than the Hyksos kingdom (18th–16th cent. B.C.E.), but at the centre of our interest are the ruins of Samaria (later called Sebastiya) — the ancient capital of Israel (882–721 B.C.E.). Founded by Omri (I Kings 16:24), Samaria today shows the ruin of his palace, along with fortifications and shrines which recall the generations when it rivalled Jerusalem and aroused the condemnation of the prophets for its blend of Jewish and pagan cultic practices. Ahab and Jezebel, against whose corruptions Elijah fought (I Kings 18:20–40), ruled in Samaria and lived in the "Ivory House" condemned by Amos (6:1–4) for symbolizing the exploitation of the poor.

When Sargon II of Assyria captured the city (722–721 B.C.E.) and deported its inhabitants, he transported thousands of settlers into Samaria from subject tribes elsewhere in his empire. Today's Samaritans claim to be descendants of Ephraim and Manasseh. But when the Temple rites were restored, the Samaritans were denied any participation. They, claiming that Abraham's offering of Isaac actually occurred on Mt. Gerizim rather than on Mount Moriah, have since that time lived in enmity with the Jerusalemites. They acknowledge the authority of no books or teachings outside the Pentateuch, maintain the rules on circumcision and avoidance of unclean foods, and each year observe Passover according to the instructions of Exodus 12:5ff at their shrine on the sacred mountain.

Unfinished Greek monastery over Jacob's Well, Shechem

The hostility between the Samaritans and the Jews is the setting of Jesus' dialogue with the Samaritan woman (John 4:5–47).

John Hyrcanus** destroyed Samaria (107 B.C.E.). Herod the Great rebuilt it as Sebaste (Augustea) in Hellenistic splendour (with theatre, forum, hippodrome, aqueduct). Justinian destroyed the city again and slaughtered the Samaritans wholesale after they had rioted, killed the Christian bishop and thousands of monks and other Christians. They never became strong again. Today they number c. 600 in two colonies (Nablus and Holon, near Tel Aviv).

There are ruins of a Roman and later Byzantine basilica (3rd cent.), and a Roman forum of the scale of the one at Caesarea*. There is also a mosque rising inside a Crusader cathedral built c. 1130.

In 1913 Joseph's Tomb (Josh. 24:32) was identified nearby, where Moses deposited the mummy of his forefather which he had transported from Egypt (Ex. 13:19). The tomb is a shrine for Jews, Samaritans, Christians and Muslims.

Jacob erected an altar here (Gen. 33:18–20), and near Joseph's Tomb is a well traditionally called "Jacob's Well." The precise location of the altar is lost: in Nablus/Shechem altars have come and gone. But in the dry country a good well is a treasure, and it draws the greatest of names to it.

SHECHEM (NABLUS)

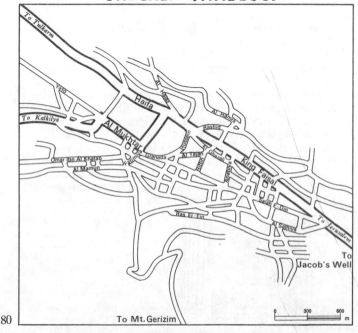

SHRINE
OF THE BOOK

Of great beauty, the Shrine of the Book at the Israel Museum in Jerusalem by its floor plan and structure evokes reflections upon the life and work of those religious and patriots who chose to live in caves rather than accommodate themselves to the pleasures and powers of what they condemned as a corrupt establishment.

Within the shrine are displayed in an imaginative way some of the documents and artifacts discovered (since 1947) in the caves along the Dead Sea (see Ein Gedi*): the "Cave of Letters," "Cave of the Pool," "Scouts' Cave," and others. Several come from Qumran, a Jewish monastic community that flourished c. 135–31 B.C.E. until destroyed by fire. Others come from the caves (excavated 1960–61) from which Jewish patriots conducted their resistance to the Roman occupation and its collaborators.

The most striking display, at the centre of the Shrine, presents the oldest full text of the book of the prophet Isaiah. Other documents discovered include the community's Manual of Discipline, the Habakkuk Commentary, the Temple Scroll, Psalms (including six not found in the Scriptures), and the Scroll of the War of the Sons of Light against the Sons of Darkness. Many of these have been translated and edited, but the scholarly unrolling and translating of others from one of the most dramatic discoveries in many centuries will go on for years to come.

An item especially interesting to Christians, whose forefathers were pacifists at that time, is an order issued by Bar Kokhba during his revolt: "I take heaven as witness against me that if any of the Galileans who are among you should be ill-treated, I will put fetters on your feet..." The "Galileans" were the Christians, still treated as a Jewish sect under Roman law, but already condemned by the rabbis of Yavneh (80 C.E.).

> The Israel Museum contains many treasures of religious significance, including exquisitely ornamented synagogue scrolls from diverse periods and places. The Billy Rose Sculpture Garden** has works by famous modern artists.
>
> Across the wadi is the Givat Ram campus of Hebrew University, with the National Library. The University's Institute of Contemporary Jewry is an important centre of study of Jewish communal life around the world, and also of the Holocaust.
>
> Nearby are the Monastery of the Cross, founded in the late 5th century by the King of Georgia (Russia) and rebuilt by Emperor Justinian, and the Knesset, with art forms created by Marc Chagall.

81

SOLOMON'S POOLS

A minor wonder, but well worth visiting, are Solomon's Pools just south of Bethlehem. Three great reservoirs carved deep into the living rock, they were once part of a marvelous system built to supply water to the Temple in Jerusalem — conveyed through eighty kilometres of conduits. From 7.6 to 13.7 metres deep, and all well over 91 metres long, they remind us again of the incredible feats of engineering and building associated with the names of the greater builders of former times in the Holy Land — Solomon, Herod, Justinian, the Crusader kings.

Their tedious and dangerous public works, which involved cutting with simple tools through great rock formations, sometimes moving and putting into place great single-cut stones the dimensions of a normal room, were executed by companies of tens of thousands of slaves.

Today one is constantly aware of the tremendous building projects going on all over Israel, and — after viewing ancient projects such as the Akko* Citadel or Solomon's Pools — he looks with fresh respect at the giant earth-moving equipment which is also seen everywhere.

Solomon's Pool

TANTUR

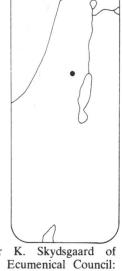

A few kilometres south of Jerusalem on the Bethlehem road is Tantur, setting for the Ecumenical Centre for Theological Studies. "Tantur" is one of the major centres of inter-church study and dialogue, and there is a steady flow of churchmen and theologians from all denominations and nations. The facilities are excellent, whether the scholar is attending a seminar for a few days or spending a sabbatical in study and writing. When he looks up from his books, the view toward Bethlehem and the Jordan Valley is superb.

"Tantur," as it is popularly known among churchmen, grew out of a suggestion made by Professor K. Skydsgaard of Copenhagen (Lutheran) during the Ecumenical Council: Vatican II. Pope Paul VI** recalled the proposal during his 1964 visit to the Holy Land and commissioned Father Theodore Hesburgh, president of the University of Notre Dame (USA) to proceed with the project.

Ultimately intended to become an international and ecumenical university, it has already (since its beginnings in 1965) attained a fine level of beauty and functionality.

Pope Paul VI

A few hundred metres away is Mar Elias**.

Mar Elias

TIBERIAS

Situated on the western shore of Lake Kinneret* is Tiberias, one of the four holy cities of Eretz Israel. Founded (1st cent. B.C.E.) by a son of Herod the Great, it is a city of many churches and synagogues, active or in ruins. At different times Tiberias has been a Christian bishopric. Under the Romans, the Muslims and the Crusaders it has been the capital of Galilee. Following the expulsion of Jews from Jerusalem it became a centre for the Sanhedrin and the patriarchs: the Jerusalem Talmud is among the religious resources prepared here, and also the system of punctuation that provided Hebrew writing with vowel signs. Here too R. Yehuda Hanasi** compiled his giant work on the Mishnah.

Within easy distance of many sites and shrines in the surrounding countryside, Tiberias today provides modern hotels from which visitors can walk through the immediate area and travel out into the hills and along the shore. On the outskirts are the ruins of the Hammath synagogue (3rd cent.), with a beautiful mosaic floor. Among the great teachers buried nearby are Maimonides (see Rambam**), R. Yohanan Ben Zakkai**, R. Isaiah Horowitz; according to tradition, R. Akiva** and his wife were also buried here.

Tiberias and Beit Shean* were foci of the efforts initiated by Don Josef** to build Jewish settlements about Lake Kinneret in the 16th century. But Tiberias today, a flourishing Jewish city surrounded by successful agricultural communities, has developed for the most part since Israel independence (1948).

Coin of Herod Antipas, struck at Tiberias

Tomb of R. Meir Ba'al ha-Nes

A short distance to the west are the hills called "the Horns of Hattin." Here the Crusader armies, marching out from Tzippori, were defeated (4 July 1187) in one of the decisive battles of history. (See also Nebi Shueib*.)

Nearby, to the south, is the tomb of the legendary R. Meir Ba'al ha-Nes. The "Meir Ba'al ha-Nes box" was once found in Jewish homes throughout Europe: into it were dropped contributions for support of the brethren in the Holy Land.

On the heights to the west are the Arbel caves, redoubts held by Jewish patriots during the Galilean revolt against King Herod's ascension to the throne (40–37 B.C.E.) and the Zealot revolt against the Roman occupation and its collaborators (66–70 C.E.). The Zealots' revolt ended in the slaughter of thousands, the selling of tens of thousands of others into slavery, and the destruction of the Temple in Jerusalem (see Western Wall*).

TIBERIAS

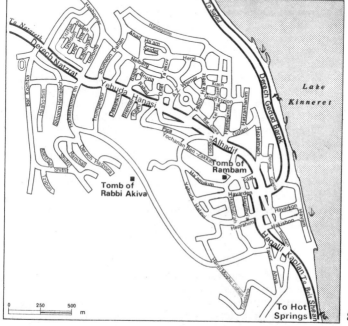

VIA DOLOROSA

St. Helena fixed to her satisfaction the location of the place of the crucifixion and Jesus' tomb (see Holy Sepulchre*). Since that time, when not impeded by wars or intolerant rulers, Christian pilgrims have come each year to retrace the path of Jesus from sentence to burial. Each incident which tradition has ascribed to that mournful course is now marked by some shrine or place of prayer.

Although many destructions and rebuildings make a direct following of Jesus' footsteps impossible, and detours are necessary, the following identifications of "the stations of the cross" are commonly made.

First: the condemnation (Matt. 27:26) — once the site of the Praetorium, now the courtyard of the El-Omariye School (Muslim).

Second: the scourging, crowning with thorns, imposition of the cross (Matt. 27:26b; 29) — by the Church of the Flagellation (Roman Catholic Franciscan; with museum).

Third: the first stumbling — Polish Roman Catholic Chapel.

Fourth: Jesus meets his mother — Armenian Catholic Church ("Our Lady of the Spasm").

Fifth: Simon Cyrene carries the cross (Matt. 27:32) — Franciscan Oratory.

Sixth: St. Veronica wipes Jesus' face — Church of St. Veronica (Greek Catholic).

Seventh: the second stumbling — formerly at the "Porta Judaica," nearby a Roman Catholic Franciscan chapel.

Eighth: Jesus' warning to the women of Jerusalem (Lk. 23:28–31) — Greek Orthodox Convent of St. Charalampos, neighbouring the Hospice of the Order of St. John (Lutheran).

Ninth: the third stumbling — Abyssinian Church and Convent of St. Anthony (Coptic).

The final five stations are within the Church of the Holy Sepulchre*.

Tenth: Jesus stripped of his garments (Matt. 27:35b) — Franciscan chapel, to the right of the nave.

Eleventh: Jesus nailed to the cross (Mk. 15:25) — the altar.

Twelfth: death on the cross (Mk. 15:37).

Thirteenth: removal of the body — statue of Mater Dolorosa (Portuguese, 1778).

Fourteenth: Jesus' body placed in the tomb of Joseph of Arimathea (Mk. 15:43–46).

The basic information is attested in the Synoptic Gospels, and reference is given here for meditation. Where no citation is given, the identification of a station depends upon Christian oral tradition.

STATIONS OF THE VIA DOLOROSA

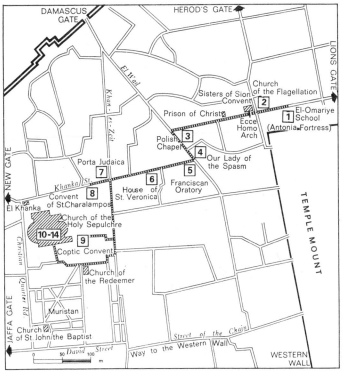

Ecce Homo arch on the Via Dolorosa

THE WESTERN WALL

In the nearly three millennia since King David (c. 1010–970 B.C.E.) made the city his capital, no city has gone through more destructions and rebuildings than Jerusalem. And no sacred place has been more splendidly honoured nor vengefully profaned than the Temple Mount. Warren's** excavations exposed 14 layers of construction and rubble (1867–70); contemporary excavations have provided a fuller understanding of the many vicissitudes and splendours of the City of David across the centuries.

For 14 centuries Jerusalem was a focus of controversy among leaders of the three large monotheistic religions. Since 1967 there has been open access for Jewish, Christian and Muslim pilgrims, guaranteed by the Israel government. Unlike its many predecessors — Roman, Persian, Umayyad, Crusader, Saracen and Mameluke and Jordanian — the State of Israel has respected the historic claims of other religions than Jewish, even when those claims conflicted with the most intense religious sentiments of Jews. Prime proof is the fact that the Muslim structures on the Temple Mount — Dome of the Rock* and El Aksa* Mosque — have been preserved and protected, even though the Mount was the site of the First and Second Temples.

The First Temple was built by King Solomon (c. 960 B.C.E.) and destroyed by the Babylonians (520 B.C.E.).

The Western Wall

Herodian stone
from the Western Wall

The Second Temple was built by the repatriates from Babylon following the First Return from Exile (c. 516 B.C.E.); devastated again by Antiochus Epiphanes, Syrian king who declared Judaism illegal (168 B.C.E.), it was restored and fortified by the Hasmonean rulers (see Alexander Yannai**) and rebuilt by Herod the Great (see Herod's Jerusalem*). With the suppression of the Zealot revolt, the Second Temple was destroyed (70 C.E.); heroic but futile resistance continued in a few ouposts like Gamla, Herodion* and Masada*, after the profanation. When heathen shrines to Jupiter, Venus and Minerva were erected by the Roman conquerors and the city renamed Aelia Capitolina (130 C.E.), another revolt started. With the suppression of Bar Kokhba's revolt (132–35 C.E.), Jews were expelled from Jerusalem and the teachers and patriarchs scattered to such temporary havens as Yavneh, Shefr'am, Usha, Beit She'arim*, Tzippori and Tiberias*. For a brief moment (361–63 C.E.) under Emperor Julian — called "the Apostate" by Christian polemicists — the Jews received permission to restore the Temple and its use, but Julian fell in war against the Persians before his policies could be implemented.

During many centuries the Temple Mount was barred to Jews, and for many seasons of Muslim control even access to the Western Wall (called "the wailing wall" during the exile before 1948) was denied. In better seasons, Jews made pilgrimage to the wall on the 9th day of the month of Av — the day of the fall of the First and Second Temples. Although free access was guaranteed by par. 8 of the 1949 armistice agreement which followed the War of Independence, the Jordanian government did not honour the agreement (and also despoiled Jewish cemeteries and synagogues in East Jerusalem).

On 7 June 1967, as the Israelis were successfully throwing back the combined forces of the Arab League attacking from the east and the south, the electric word was flashed by Israeli parachutists to command HQ: "The Temple Mount is ours. I repeat: the Temple Mount is ours!" A quarter of a million people flocked to the Western Wall, to celebrate — and to pray — without harassment.

89

YAD VASHEM

A generation had to pass before people — except a few poets and novelists and solitary scholars — could begin to confront the Holocaust and the lessons of the Holocaust. To the Jews, the murder of one-third of their people in the heart of Christendom was a trauma of epochal proportions. To the Christians, whether perpetrators or spectators, confrontation with the Holocaust put their profession of faith to the question. As happened with the Exodus and Sinai, and other events that have shaped religious history, a generation had to pass ("forty years in the wilderness" — Num. 14:31–33, Deut. 8:2) before Jews and Christians could begin to study and to teach the meanings of the *sho'ah.*

In the meantime a few devoted people were working to gather the records of the destroyed villages and families, to record the testimonies of survivors, to provide places for remembering the sacrifice. Chief among these memorials is Yad Vashem, on the outskirts of Jerusalem. The buildings of Yad Vashem house extensive archives and a library, research facilities and editorial offices, an exhibit of the death camps and their victims, and an impressive memorial building with an eternal light. On the floor of black stone are engraved the names of the killing places: Auschwitz, Treblinka, Sobibor, Maidanek, Bergen-Belsen... "To have faith is to remember!"

Righteous of the Nations medal

In the park surrounding the buildings is a children's memorial, featuring a relief sculpture of the children and Janusz Korczak**, who went with those who had trusted him rather than accept reprieve by abandoning them in their hour of greatest need. Surrounding the park are more than 26,000 trees, planted in the Avenue of the Righteous Gentiles — each individual tree with a plaque citing some person (Dutch, Belgian, French, German, Polish, Bulgarian...) who has been proven to have saved one or more Jews from death at the hands of the Nazis and their collaborators. The number is small, considering the statistical claims of the churches in the so-called Christian nations, but it is large enough to make a footnote to the Holocaust — a candle to light the darkness in a genocidal era of human history.

Memorial by Boris Saktsier of Janusz Korczak and the children of the ghetto

A shrine to the 6,000,000 victims of Bergen-Belsen and other camps is found on Mount Zion: Martef HaSho'ah (f. 1949).

Other memorials with museums and archives are Lohamei Hagetaot*, north of Akko*, and Yad Mordechai**, south of Jaffa-Tel Aviv*.

At Tel Yitzhak** there is a school for training teachers of the Holocaust. There are also research programmes and seminars at the universities in Haifa, Tel Aviv, Jerusalem and Beer Sheva.

North of Beit Shemesh, near Mesilat Tzion, is a Martyrs' Forest and Memorial Grotto, founded in 1959 by the B'nei B'rith International.

YEHI'AM

During the 10th and 11th centuries a peace crusade spread across European Christendom, impelled in part by field preachers who went forth from monasteries purified and renewed by a reform movement. Under the "Truce of God" and "Peace of God" they strove to bring the princelings and robber barons of barbarous and illiterate tribes under some restraints: certain categories of persons — nuns, doctors, priests, monks, nurses — were to be spared in the incessant wars, sieges and battles; certain seasons of the church calendar — Advent, Lent, certain Saints' Days — were to be times when fighting was prohibited. The task of the Christian teachers was difficult: Islamic conquest had torn away more than half of Christendom, including almost all of the ancient centres of Christian education and culture — by far the better half. The rump that remained formally Christian, or was open to missionary work, was largely illiterate, superstitious, polygamous — and constantly engaged in banditry and tribal warfare.

The message that launched the Crusades at the Council of Clermont (1096), preached by Peter the Hermit (1050?–1115?) in the First Crusade and Bernard of Clairvaux (1091–1153) in the Second Crusade, was simple and direct: if you must fight, cease fighting fellow-Christians; fight to free the Holy Places from the Muslim defilers. Back of this message was a monolithic view of the Good Society (Christian), and there followed bad years for those who didn't fit. The Crusaders pillaged and murdered in the Jewish communities en route to embarkation points. Church authorities blessed both the external crusades, and also internal crusades against Christian dissidents (Albigenses, Waldenses and Bogomili). The Inquisition was founded to enforce conformity by torture, fire and sword, and its cruelties were suffered by both Jews and non-conforming Christians.

Adventurers swarmed to the Crusader banners, from lesser nobles to landless peasants. Even kings and emperors were in time involved. The church promised heaven to those who died fighting the enemy and hell to those who persisted in fighting fellow-Christians. In the combined economic, political and religious motivation, the crusade served all interests and unleashed all passions. When Jerusalem was captured (1099), the slaughter of the Jewish and Muslim inhabitants extended from the defenders on the walls to women and children in the alleys and back rooms.

Yet there was a constructive side to the vision of a re-Christianized Holy Land, expressed at the level of which churchmen and warriors were then capable. Where Constantine and Justinian had once built, magnificent new churches were constructed at the Holy Places. Old monastic centres were restored in personnel and quarters. Great castles were constructed or rebuilt, from Krak des Chevaliers (now in Syria) to St. Catherine's Monastery* at the foot of Mount Sinai, which still inspire wonder though most are in ruins.

Judin Castle

Yehi'am (Judin Castle) and Montfort, just four kilometres apart and guarding the approach from Damascus to the port of Akko*, may be taken as representative of the fortifications that extended — about a day's journey by horse apart — south into the Negev, along the Mediterranean to Jaffa* and the old Philistine cities, and along the Dead Sea to the Red Sea. Castle Judin was built by the Knights Templar and transferred to the Teutonic Knights; it was captured and demolished by Baybars in 1265. Montfort (Starkenburg) was captured and destroyed in 1271. A few years later Akko fell, and the last of the Crusader forces debarked from Atlit — the only fortification never captured by the Saracens — for Europe. In 1291 there ended nearly two centuries of Crusader kingdoms in the Holy Land.

Many of the ruined fortifications, their locations originally chosen to command the surrounding countryside, afford magnificent views. Belvoir ("Beautiful View," though in Hebrew a new name was given — "Star of the Jordan"), north of Beit Shean*, like Yehi'am and Montfort a restored and supervised historic site, is also worth visiting. From its vantage today one looks out over the fertile fields and carp pools of peaceful and prosperous agricultural settlements in the Jordan Valley.

The battle at the Horns of Hattin, the mountain heights just west of Tiberias*, marked the closing of this book of Holy Land history. Here Saladin (see Salah ad-Din**) kept the Crusader forces, with their heavy coats of mail and huge horses, waiting through the heat of the day — and then with his fleet and lightly clad cavalry delivered the swift and fatal blow against thirsty, dispirited and out-maneuvered adversaries (4 July 1187).

With the exception of Napoleon's brief and futile sortie in 1798–99, the Christian nations played no significant political or military role in the Near East again until the collapse of the Ottoman Empire during World War I.

HISTORICAL MAPS

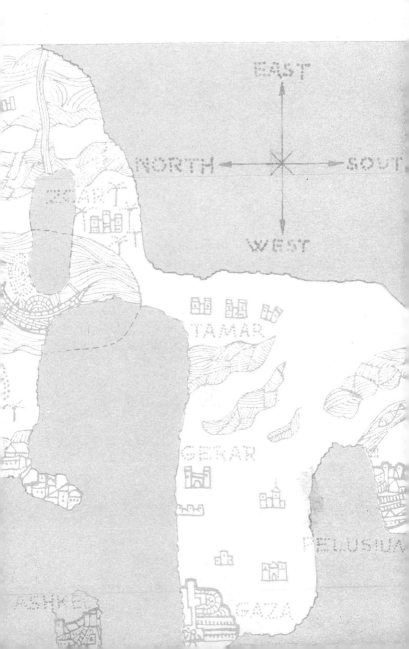

Hamath

Orontes R.

Lebo-hamath

Damascus

Mediterranean Sea

Hazor

Dor

Megiddo

Jordan R.

Tell Qasile
Joppa

Gezer

Ekron

Jerusalem

Ashdod

Beth-shemesh

Ashkelon

Gath

Gaza

PHILISTINES

Ashan

Arad

Beer-sheba

Baalath-beer

Rabbah

Hazar-addar

Jotbathah

Timna

Elath
(Ezion-geber)

0   50   100
k m

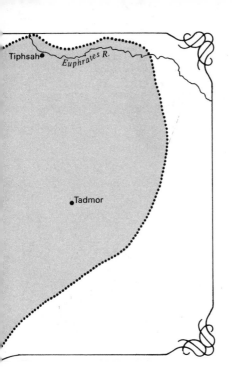

Tiphsah
Euphrates R.

•Tadmor

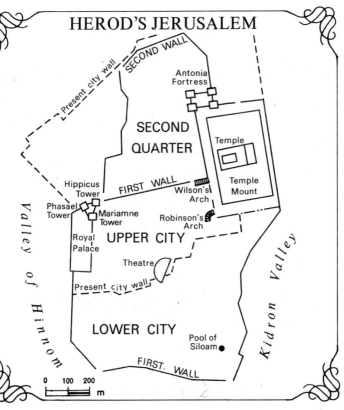

HEROD'S JERUSALEM

Present city wall

SECOND WALL

Antonia Fortress

SECOND QUARTER

Temple

FIRST WALL

Hippicus Tower

Wilson's Arch

Temple Mount

Phasael Tower

Mariamne Tower

Robinson's Arch

Royal Palace

UPPER CITY

Valley of Hinnom

Theatre

Present city wall

Kidron Valley

LOWER CITY

Pool of Siloam

FIRST WALL

FIRST WALL

0   100   200
m

Coin of Herod the Great

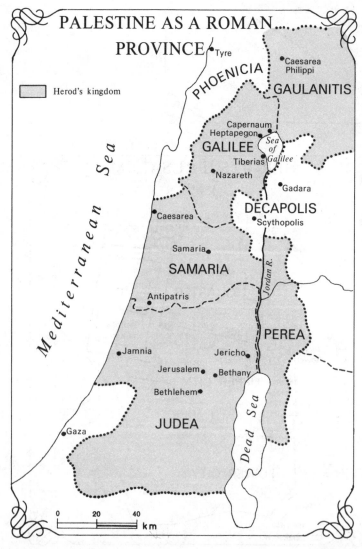

PALESTINE AS A ROMAN PROVINCE

Herod's kingdom

Tyre

PHOENICIA

Caesarea
Philippi

GAULANITIS

Capernaum
Heptapegon

Sea of Galilee

GALILEE

Tiberias

Nazareth

Gadara

Caesarea

DECAPOLIS

Scythopolis

Samaria

SAMARIA

Jordan R.

Antipatris

PEREA

Jamnia

Jericho

Jerusalem
Bethany

Bethlehem

Dead Sea

Gaza

JUDEA

Mediterranean Sea

0   20   40
km

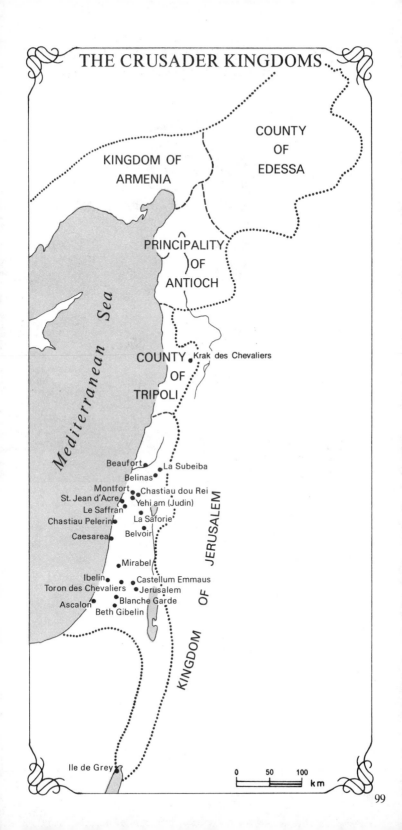

THE CRUSADER KINGDOMS

COUNTY OF EDESSA

KINGDOM OF ARMENIA

PRINCIPALITY OF ANTIOCH

Mediterranean Sea

COUNTY OF TRIPOLI

Krak des Chevaliers

Beaufort • • La Subeiba
Belinas •
Montfort • • Chastiau dou Rei
St. Jean d'Acre • • Yehi am (Judin)
Le Saffran • • La Saforie
Chastiau Pelerin •
Caesarea • • Belvoir

KINGDOM OF JERUSALEM

• Mirabel

Ibelin • • Castellum Emmaus
Toron des Chevaliers • • Jerusalem
Ascalon • • Blanche Garde
Beth Gibelin

KINGDOM OF JERUSALEM

Ile de Grey

0   50   100
k m

99

ERETZ ISRAEL AS A PROVINCE OF THE OTTOMAN EMPIRE

ROMANIA 1908

YUGOSLAVIA 1918

BULGARIA 1878

ALBANIA 1913

GREECE 1830

Constantinople

TURKEY Republic 1915

SYRIA 1946

LEBANON 1946
Beirut

Mediterranean Sea

Jerusalem British Mandate of Palestine (1921)

LIBYA 1951

Cairo

Sinai to Egypt 1910

EGYPT 1922

Nile R.

ARABIA 1916

0   200   400
km

1946 Date of independence

Ottoman Empire 1830

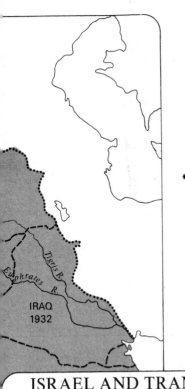

* Palestine was the term used by
the Romans, Byzantines and
Arabs; the Crusaders and
Ottomans used other terminology;
"Palestine" became a political
term again with the British
Mandate (1921)

IRAQ
1932

ISRAEL AND TRANSJORDAN 1948

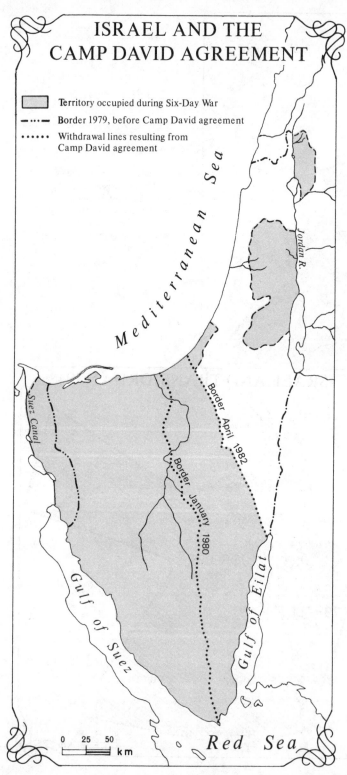

ISRAEL AND THE CAMP DAVID AGREEMENT

Territory occupied during Six-Day War

Border 1979, before Camp David agreement

Withdrawal lines resulting from
Camp David agreement

Mediterranean Sea

Jordan R.

Suez Canal

Border April 1982

Border January 1980

Gulf of Suez

Gulf of Eilat

0   25   50
km

Red Sea

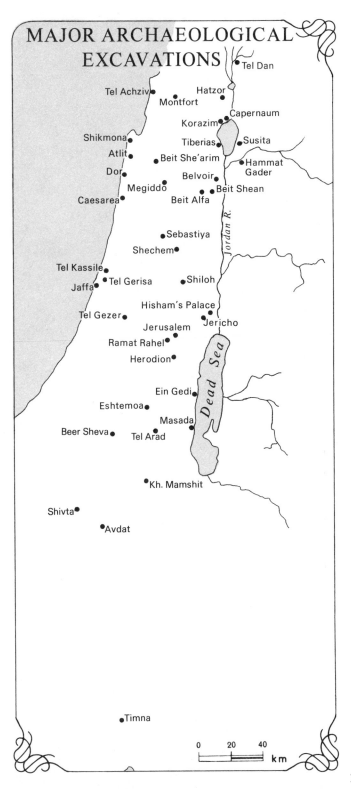

MAJOR ARCHAEOLOGICAL EXCAVATIONS

Tel Dan

Tel Achziv · · Hatzor
Montfort ·
· Capernaum
Korazim · ·
Shikmona · · Tiberias · Susita
Atlit · · Beit She'arim · Hammat
Gader
Dor · · Belvoir
Megiddo · · Beit Shean
Caesarea · Beit Alfa

· Sebastiya
Shechem ·

Tel Kassile ·
Jaffa · · Tel Gerisa · Shiloh

Tel Gezer · Hisham's Palace ·
Jerusalem · · Jericho
Ramat Rahel ·
Herodion ·

Ein Gedi ·
Eshtemoa · *Dead Sea*
Masada ·
Beer Sheva · Tel Arad

· Kh. Mamshit

Shivta ·
· Avdat

Jordan R.

· Timna

0   20   40
k m

CATALOGUE OF PERSONS
Memorialized in Names of
Streets, Settlements and
Institutions

Names with the definite article Al, Ad, At, etc. are alphabetized under the name proper.

Aaronsohn family of pioneers: father a founder of Zichron Ya'akov; brother (Aaron: 1876–1919) discovered wild wheat at Rosh Pina; sister (Sarah: 1890–1917), heroine who died working in Nili, the Jewish intelligence network assisting the British in WWI

S. Aaronsohn

Aba Sinan see **Ibn Sina**

Abba Hillel see **Silver**

Abba Sikra/Sakkara (1st cent.), a leader of Zealots' revolt against the Roman occupation

Abdullah Abdullah Ibn Husein (1882–1951), king of Transjordan after independence (1946)

Abrabanel Isaac Abrabanel (1437–1508), Bible commentator and philosopher; statesman in courts of Spain, Portugal, Italy

Abraham, House of R.C. Benedictine centre on Mount of Offence, Jerusalem; see Avraham Avinu**

Abu Bakhr (573–634), successor to Muhammed and first caliph

Abulafia R. Hayyim Nissim Ben Isaac Abulafia (1775–1861), leader in Tiberias, Damascus and Jerusalem (Chief Rabbi)

Adam HaKohen pseudonym for Abraham Dov Lebensohn (1794–1878), Hebrew poet and teacher in Vilna, leader in the Russian *Haskalah* (Enlightenment)

Adani R. Shlomo Bar Yehoshua Adani (1567–1625), Mishnah commentator, leader of Jewish community of Yemen

Adoniyahu R. Adoniyahu HaCohen; came to Jerusalem in 1900; leader of Persian community

Agan acronym for R. Avraham Haim Gagin (1787–1848), Chief Rabbi of Eretz Israel, first one to be authorized by a Turkish firman

Agmon Nathan (Agmon) Bistritsky (b. 1896), author and translator; leader in Jewish National Fund

Agnon Shmuel Yosef Agnon (1888–1970), Hebrew poet and novelist; Nobel Laureate in Literature (1966)

Agrippas Agrippa I (10 B.C.E.–44 C.E.), king of Judah; built 3rd wall of Jerusalem

Agron Gershon Agronsky (1894–1959), journalist (f. *Palestine Post*, now *The Jerusalem Post*); mayor of Jerusalem

Ahad Ha'am pseudonym for Asher Zvi Ginzberg (1856–1927), writer, leader in Hoveve Zion; opponent of political Zionism and champion of cultural Zionism

Aharonovitch Yosef Aharonovitch (1887–1937), writer and editor (*HaPo'el HaTza'ir*); director of Bank HaPo'alim ("the workers' bank")

Ahima'az Biblical Ahimaaz, runner and would-be messenger (II Sam. 18:22–30)

Ahinoam wife of King Saul and mother of Jonathan (I Sam. 14:49–50)

Al-Akhtal Ghiat at-Taghlibi al-Akhtal (640?–710?), popular name of Christian Arab poet under the Umayyads

Akiva R. Akiva Ben Yosef (c. 50–135), chief teacher who decisively influenced development of *Halakha*; martyred at time of Bar Kokhba revolt

Albaz R. Moses Ben Maimon Albaz (16th cent.), Moroccan Kabbalist and writer (*Heikhal Kodesh*)

Albright Institute of Oriental Research, Jerusalem William Foxwell Albright (1891–1971), archaeologist and writer (*From the Stone Age to Christianity*, 1940); professor at Johns Hopkins University

Alfasi R. Isaac Ben Jacob Alfasi (1013–1103), author of most important code prior to *Mishneh Torah* of Maimonides

Alharizi Judah Ben Solomon al-Harizi (1170–1235), Hebrew poet, translator, musical historian

Alkabez R. Solomon Ben Moses HaLevi Alkabez (1505–76), Kabbalist, mystical poet (*Lekhah Dodi*); Bible commentator and teacher (incl. M. Cordovero) in Safad

Alkalai R. Judah Solomon Hai Alkalai (1798–1878), writer, precursor of modern Zionism

Allenby Edmund Henry Hynman Allenby (1861–1936), British general and viscount, liberator of Jerusalem in WWI

Allon Gedalya Allon (1901–50), historian and professor at Hebrew University

Alonei Yitzhak youth village S.E. of Zichron Ya'akov, named for Yitzhak Gruenbaum**

Alroy David Alroy/Menahem Ben Solomon (12th cent.), leader of a messianic movement in Kurdistan; fiction by Disraeli — *Wondrous Tales of Alroy* (1839)

Alshekh R. Moses Alshekh (16th cent.), Talmudist and Bible commentator in Safad; pupil of R. Joseph Caro**

Alterman Nathan Alterman (1910–70), Israel poet, playwright and translator; contributed to *Ha'aretz, Davar*

N. Alterman

Aluf David see **Marcus**

Aluf Sadeh see **Sadeh**

Aluf Simhoni see **Simhoni**

Amiel R. Moshe Avigdor Amiel (1882–1945), leader in Mizrahi; a founder of Tahkemoni School; Chief Rabbi of Tel Aviv

Aminadav Biblical Amminadab, ancestor of King David (Ruth 4:20)

Amon king of Judah (642–640 B.C.E.)

Amos prophet (8th cent. B.C.E.); see book of Amos in Bible

Amram Ga'on Amram Ben Sheshna (9th cent.), *gaon* of Sura

Anielewicz Mordecai Anielewicz (1919–43), leader in HaShomer HaTza'ir; commander of the Warsaw ghetto uprising

M. Anielewicz

Antigonus (80?–37 B.C.E.); last of the Hasmonean kings of Judah; defeated and killed by the Romans

Aqabat Shaddad named for Shaddad Ben Avs (d. 677), friend of Omar Ibn al-Khattab**

Ariel Dov Ariel (1860–1943), Bilu pioneer, a founder of Gedera

Arlosoroff Hayim Victor Arlosoroff (1899–1933), leader in HaPo'el HaTza'ir (ed. *Die Arbeit*), WZO, Jewish Agency, Va'ad Leumi; a founder of Hitahadut (1920)

Asahel Biblical figure (II Sam. 3:27–39)

Ashdot Ya'akov *kibbutzim* "A" and "B" near Lake Kinneret; Ya'akov refers to James de Rothschild**

Asher son of patriarch Jacob (Gen. 30:12–13), forerunner of one of the 12 tribes of Israel

Ashlag R. Judah Leib Ashlag (1886–1955), Kabbalist, author of *The Ladder* (extensive translation and commentary on *Zohar* and *Zohar Kodesh*)

Assaf Simha Assaf (1899–1953), professor and rector of Hebrew University; leader in Mizrahi; Supreme Court justice

Ath-Athma Yusuf ath-Athma (1884–1920), Turkish officer in WWI

Auerbach Elias Auerbach (1882–1971), Israel Bible scholar; author of *Wueste und Gelobtes Land*

Auerbach R. Ephraim Auerbach (d. 1948), a founder of Beit Israel

Augusta Victoria Hospital opened in 1910 and named for Augusta Victoria (1858–1921), wife of Kaiser Wilhelm II

Auster Square Daniel Auster (1893–1962), mayor of Jerusalem 1936–38, 1944–45, 1948–51

Avigail Biblical Abigail (I Sam. 25:3)

Avigdor *moshav* f. 1950 near Kiriyat Mal'achi; see Avigdor Eshet**

Avigdor Eshet Sir Osmond D'Avigdor-Goldsmid (1877–1940), British public leader; chairman of Jewish Colonization Association

Avimelech Abimelech, king of Gerar (Gen. 21:22–32)

Avner Abner, commander of Saul's army (I Sam. 14:50); opposed David, killed by Joab (II Sam. 2–3)

Avner Ben Ner see **Avner**

Avraham Avinu "Abraham our Father;" Biblical patriarch who received the promises (Gen. 13:14–17; 15:7–21)

Azar Samuel Bekhor Azar (d. 1954), a teacher sentenced to death with Max Bennett and Moshe Marzouk in Cairo trial

Azriel *moshav* S.E. of Netanya, f. 1951; see Hildesheimer**

Ba'al Shem-Tov Israel Ben Eliezer Ba'al Shem-Tov (1700?–60), healer and teacher; founder of modern Hasidism

Bacher R. Nisim Bacher (1848–1931), teacher and Sephardic leader in Jerusalem

Badhav R. Isaac Ben Michael Badhav (1859–1947), scholar in Jerusalem

Baharan R. Shlomo Zalman Baharan (1838–1910), traditionalist; founder of Mea She'arim sector of Jerusalem

Bak R. Nisan Bak (1815–89), a founder of Hasidism in Jerusalem and communal leader

Balaban R. Meir Balaban (1877–1942), historian (*History of the Jewish People*); teacher (Jewish high school in Czestochowa, rabbinical seminary Tahkemoni in Warsaw); director of Institute for Jewish Studies in Warsaw

Balfour Lord Arthur James Balfour (1848–1930), British statesman; author of Balfour Declaration (2 November 1917)

Lord Balfour

Balfouriya *moshav* f. 2 November 1922 near Nazareth; see Balfour**

Barak military leader in the time of the Judges, who defeated Sisera of Hatzor (Judg. 4:16; 5:1)

Barash Asher Barash (1889–1952), writer, president of Hebrew Writers' Association

Bar Giora Simeon Bar Giora, military leader in war against Roman occupation (66–70 C.E.)

Bar-Ilan R. Meir Bar-Ilan (1880–1949), leader in Mizrahi; educator

109

Bar-Ilan University f. 1955 under auspices of Religious Zionists of America, named for R. Bar-Ilan**

Bar Kokhba Simeon Bar Kokhba (d. 135), leader of revolt (132–35) against Roman occupation

Bar Nissan Yosef Katznelson (1890–1940), a founder of Etzel; organizer of illegal immigration from Poland before the Holocaust

Bartenura see **Obadiah MiBertinoro**

Bar-Yehuda Israel Bar-Yehuda (1895–1965), leader in Histadrut; member of Knesset and Cabinet

Bar Yohai see **Shimon**

Bar Yohai settlement W. of Safad, named for Shimon Bar Yohai**

Barzilai Joshua Barzilai (Eisenstat: 1855–1918), writer and communal leader; a founder of Jerusalem Hebrew high school and of Beit Ha'am Centre

Bavli R. Menahem Ben Moses Bavli (fl. 16th cent.), Kabbalist and leader in Safad and Hebron

Bayt Shmuel Bayt (1902–48), manager of *aliyah* from Germany

Be'eri kibbutz S. of Gaza, f. 1946, named for B. Katznelson**

Be'erot Yitzhak kibbutz E. of Tel Aviv, f. 1948, named for I. Nissenbaum**

Beilinson Moshe Beilinson (1890–1936), writer; leader in Histadrut and Mapai

Beit Berl school of Labour Party near Kfar Sava, named for B. Katznelson**

Beit Ezra *moshav* near Ashkelon, f. 1950, named for Biblical scribe Ezra**

Beit Gail centre f. 1980 by Nature Protection Society at kibbutz Ma'agan Michael**, named for Gail Rubin, nature photographer murdered by terrorists 11 March 1978

Beit Gamliel *moshav* S.W. of Rehovot, f. 1949, named for R. Gamaliel the Younger; see Ben Gamaliel**

Beit Gordon Museum for Nature and Agriculture at kibbutz Degania, named for A.D. Gordon**

Beit Halevi *moshav* E. of Ra'anana, f. 1945 by Sephardim, named for Yehuda Halevi**

Beit Hananya *moshav* N. of Hadera, f. 1950, named for Hananya Gottlieb, head of PICA

Beit Hillel *moshav* E. of Kiriyat Shmona, f. 1940, named for H. Joffe**

Beit Meir *moshav* W. of Jerusalem, f. 1950, named for M. Bar-Ilan**

Beit Meir HQ building of Mizrahi in Jerusalem, named for M. Bar-Ilan**

Beit Nehemia *moshav* near Lod, f. 1950, named for Nehemiah**

Beit Nir kibbutz near Kiriyat Gat, f. 1955, named for M. (Nir) Bodenheimer**

Beit Uziel   *moshav* S. of Ramla, f. 1956, named for R. Uziel**

Beit Yannai   *moshav* N. of Netanya, f. 1933, named for Alexander Yannai**

Beit Yehoshua   *moshav* S. of Netanya, f. 1938, named for R. Osias (Yehoshua) Thon (1870–1936), writer and Polish Zionist leader

Beit Yitzhak   *moshav* E. of Tel Aviv, f. 1940, named for I. Feuerring**

Beit Yosef   *moshav* N. of Beit Shean, f. 1937; named for Y. Aharonovitch**

Beit Zeid   see **Giv'ot Zeid**

Belkind   Israel Belkind (1861–1929), a founder of Bilu immigration movement

Belzer   Hasidic rabbinical dynasty, origin Belz in Galicia: Shalom Roke'ah (1779–1855); Joshua Dov (1825–94); Isaachar Dov (1854–1927); Aaron Dov (1880–1957); Issachar Dov (b. 1948), founder of Beit Midrash in Jerusalem

Ben-Ami   Mordecai (Rabinovitz) Ben-Ami (1854–1932), story writer and leader in Hoveve Zion

Ben-Ami   *moshav* near Nahariya, f. 1949, named for Ben-Ami Pechter (d. 1948), who fell in War of Independence

Ben-Avi   Ithamar Ben-Avi (1882–1943), Hebrew writer and journalist (f. *Do'ar HaYom* and ed. *Palestine Weekly*)

I. Ben-Avi

Ben-David   Lazarus Ben-David (1762–1832), German Jewish philosopher and editor, a leader in *Haskalah* rationalism

Ben-Dor   Isaac Ben-Dor (1893–1948), journalist and labour leader

Ben-Eliezer   Arieh Ben-Eliezer (b. 1913), leader in Histadrut; member of Knesset

Ben Gamaliel   R. Gamaliel the Younger (d. 115), grandson of Hillel; head of Sanhedrin at Yavneh

Ben-Gavriel   Moshe Ya'akov Ben-Gavriel (1891–1965), author and Zionist

Ben-Gurion   David (Green) Ben-Gurion (1886–1973), writer, editor (*HaAgdut*); statesman; leader in Po'ale Zion, Histadrut, Mapai, Va'ad Leumi, Jewish Agency, Haganah; 1st prime minister, 1st defence minister

Ben-Gurion Airport,   near Lod

Ben-Gurion University,   Beer Sheva*

Ben-Gurion Archives and Museum,   Sde Boker*

Ben Labrat   Donash Ben Labrat (10th cent.), Jewish poet in Spain

Ben Maimon   R. Moses Maimonides; see Rambam**

Ben Matitiyahu Joseph Ben Matthias/Josephus Flavius (37?–100), Jewish commander and historian (*The Jewish War*)

Ben Perahyah R. Daniel Ben Perahyah HaKohen (d. 1575), *yeshiva* head in Salonica (Greece)

Ben Shetah Simeon Ben Shetah (1st cent. B.C.E.), scholar and Sanhedrin leader

Ben Sira Simeon Ben Jesus Ben Sira (2nd cent. B.C.E.), Hebrew sage (author of *Ecclesiastes*)

Ben Uzziel R. Jonathan Ben Uzziel (1st cent. B.C.E.–1st cent. C.E.), pupil of Hillel; translated Prophets into Aramaic

Ben Ya'ir Eliezer Ben Ya'ir (d. 73 C.E.), commander of Masada

Ben-Yehuda Eliezer Ben-Yehuda (1858–1922), teacher who updated and launched Hebrew as a modern language; edited monumental dictionary

E. Ben-Yehuda

Ben Zakkai R. Johanan Ben Zakkai (1st cent.), founder of centre of learning at Yavneh after destruction of the Temple (70 C.E.)

Ben Zakkai *moshav* near Tel Aviv, f. 1949, named for R. Ben Zakkai**

Ben-Zvi Yitzhak Ben-Zvi (1884–1963), 2nd president of Israel; leader of Histadrut; president of Va'ad Leumi

Berditchev Abba Berditchev (1918–44), parachutist captured and killed in Slovakia in WWII

Berdyczewski see **Bin-Gorion**

Berenice wife of Aristobulus, Hasmonean king; mother of Herod Agrippa I (King of Judea: 41–44 C.E.)

Berenice

Berlin R. Chaim Berlin (1832–1913), head of Etz Hayim *yeshiva* in Jerusalem

Bernstein Peretz Bernstein (1890–1971), leader in Jewish Agency, General Zionist Party; member of Knesset and Cabinet

Besht see **Ba'al Shem-Tov**

Bezalel Bezalel Ben Uri, builder of the Tabernacle (Ex. 35:30–35; 36–39)

Bialik Hayyim Nahman Bialik (1873–1934), national poet of Eretz Israel; translator, editor (*HaShilo'ah*), publisher (f. Dvir)

Billy Rose Sculpture Garden William Samuel Rosenberg (1899–1966), American songwriter and showman

Bin-Gorion Micha Yosef Bin-Gorion (1865–1921), Hebrew novelist, essayist, editor

Bin Nun see **Yehoshua Bin Nun**

Binyamina village S. of Zichron Ya'akov, f. 1922, named for Benjamin Edmond de Rothschild**

Binyamin Mitudela R. Benjamin Ben-Jonah of Tudela (fl. 1159–72), traveller (incl. Eretz Israel) and writer (*Itinerary*)

Binyamin Rabbi popular name of Yehoshua Radler-Feldman (1880–1957), editor (*HaMe'orer, HaHed*) and translator; leader in WZO, Mizrahi, and B'rit Shalom

Biram Arthur (Yizhak) Biram (1878–1967), Hebrew educator, head of Reali high school in Haifa (1920–48)

Birnbaum Nathan Birnbaum (1864–1937), writer, originator of term "Zionism," leader in Hoveve Zion, Agudat Israel

Bitan Aharon *moshav* N. of Netanya, f. 1936, named for Archibald Jacob (Aharon) Freiman, Canadian Zionist leader

Blau R. Moshe Blau (1885–1946), editor (*Kol Yisrael*); leader in Agudat Israel

Blaustein Jacob Blaustein (1892–1970), U.S. industrialist and philanthropist; president of American Jewish Committee 1949–54

Bloch R. Josef Samuel Bloch (1850–1923), editor, member of Austrian parliament, vigorous opponent of antisemitism

Bnei Aiyish rural settlement E. of Ashdod, f. 1958, named for Akiba Josef Schlesinger (1837–1922), religious Zionist

Bnei Re'em *moshav* E. of Ashdod, f. 1949, named for rabbi of Gora Kalwaria: Abraham Mordecai Alter (1864–1948)

Boaz Biblical figure; see book of Ruth

Bodenheimer Max Isidor Bodenheimer (1865–1940), associate of Herzl**, director of Jewish National Fund 1907–14

Bograshov Hayim Bograshov (1876–1963), pioneer and teacher (f. Herzliya high school in Tel Aviv); Knesset member

Bolivar Simon Bolivar (1783–1830), South American liberator (Venezuela, Colombia, Peru)

Borochov Dov Ber Borochov (1881–1917), theoretician of Socialist Zionism ("Our Platform," 1906); founder of Po'ale Zion; a leader in Zionist Congresses; editor (*Die Warheit*); historian and encyclopedist (*The Library of the Jewish Philologist*)

Botta Paul-Emile Botta (1802–70), French archaeologist and diplomat

Bracha Fuld see **Fuld**

Brachyahu Aharon Michael Brachyahu (1870–1946), chairman of Hebrew Teachers Union; a founder of Beit Hakerem

Brandeis Louis Dembitz Brandeis (1856–1941), foremost American Zionist leader 1914–21; U.S. Supreme Court Justice 1916–39

Braude R. Markus (Mordekhai Ze'ev) Braude (1869–1949), early Galician Zionist

Brenner Joseph Hayim Brenner (1881–1921), Hebrew and Yiddish author, editor (*HaAdamah*) and translator; a founder of Histadrut

Brodetsky Selig Brodetsky (1888–1954), mathematician; president of British Board of Deputies and member of Jewish Agency Executive 1939–42

Brody R. Heinrich (Hayyım) Brody (1868–1942), bibliographer; editor and publisher of Hebrew poetry; head of Schocken Institute

Bronfman Centre Edgar Bronfman (b. 1929), American Jewish communal leader and philanthropist

Bruria Beruryah (2nd cent.), daughter of R. Hananiah Ben Teradyon, wife of R. Meir; famous for her knowledge and *halakhic* teaching

Buber Martin Buber (1878–1965), leader of Frankfurt Lehrhaus (1933–38); associate of Magnes** in Ihud and professor at Hebrew University; philosophical writer, including *I and Thou* (1958)

Burla Yehuda Burla (1886–1969), Hebrew novelist; leader in Histadrut

Busal R. Hayyim Ben Jacob Obadiah de Busal (d. 1565?), Kabbalist in Salonica (Greece)

Bustenai Bustenai Ben Hanini (c. 618–70), 1st exilarch in Babylonia after the Arab conquest

Carlebach Ezriel Carlebach (1908–56), writer and journalist; founder of *Ma'ariv* (1948)

Carmia see **Cremieux**

Caro R. Josef Ben Ephraim Caro (1488–1575), Kabbalist and leader in Safad community; head of large *yeshiva*; author of authoritative code of orthodox Jewry, *Shulhan Arukh*, and of *Kesef Mishneh*

Chasanowich Joseph Chasanowich (1844–1919), Bialystok supporter of Herzl**; founder of Jewish National Library

Chopin Frederic Francois Chopin (1810–49), composer and pianist

Cohen Eliyahu Ben Saul Cohen (1924–65), famous Israeli espionage agent in Syria

Cohen Ephraim Cohen (1863–1943), educator in Jerusalem

Cremieux Isaac Adolphe Cremieux (1796–1880), French Jew active in revolution of 1848 and Paris Commune (1870–71); Deputy and Cabinet member; a founder of Alliance Israelite Universelle (1858)

Daniel   Daniel Ben Azariah, *gaon* of Palestine (1051–62)

Daniel   prophet, see Biblical book of Daniel

Dankner   Moshe Dankner (b. 1898), merchant and Haganah leader

David   see **David Hamelech**

David Hamelech   King David (1013?–973? B.C.E.), king of Judah and Israel, who moved the capital from Hebron to Jerusalem ("the City of David"); to him are attributed many Psalms; see also I Sam. 17:12 to I Kings 2:12, I Chron. 11–29

Davidson   Israel Davidson (1870–1939), scholar of medieval Hebrew literature; professor at Jewish Theological Seminary (NYC)

Deborah   prophetess (Judg. 4–5)

De Haas   Jacob De Haas (1872–1937), writer and editor; represented Herzl** in USA (leader in ZOA); later associate of Jabotinsky** and Revisionists

Demetrius, St.   4th century Christian saint

Dessler   R. Elijah Eliezer Dessler (1891–1954), leader in the Musar movement (Gateshead, England *yeshiva* and Ponevezh *yeshiva* in Bnei Berak, Israel)

Devora   see **Deborah**

Devora   *moshav* S. of Afula, f. 1956, named for Biblical Deborah**

Ad-Din   Jalal ad-Din (d. 1231), Muslim ruler who fought armies of Genghis Khan

Diskin   R. Moses Joshua Judah Leib Diskin (1817–98), orthodox leader ("the Brisker Rav") in Jerusalem

Diskin Orphanage,   Old City, Jerusalem

Disraeli   Benjamin Disraeli (1804–81), writer (*Alroy, Tancred*); British statesman and prime minister

B. Disraeli

Dizengoff   Meir Dizengoff (1861–1936), leader in Hoveve Zion; a founder and longtime mayor of Tel Aviv

Don Josef   Joseph Nasi (c. 1524–79), a Marrano; advisor to Suleiman I and Selim II; sponsor of Jewish settlement in Tiberias and vicinity

Dori   Ya'akov Dori (1899–1973), first chief of staff of Haganah and IDF; president of the Technion (1951–65)

Dostai   Bar Yehuda Dostai (2nd cent.), Talmudic scholar

Dreyfus   Alfred Dreyfus (1859–1935), a Jew and French General Staff officer; victim in famous antisemitic case, rehabilitated after 14 years

Dubnow Simon Dubnow (1860–1941), historian; theoretician of *galut* nationalism

S. Dubnow

Efraim Ephraim, 2nd son of Joseph (Gen. 41:52)

Ehrlich Paul Ehrlich (1854–1915), pioneer in chemotherapy and immunology; discoverer of "606" (Salvarsan); 1908 Nobel Prize winner

Ehud Biblical Ehud, 2nd judge of Israelites (Judg. 3:15)

Ein Hanatziv kibbutz S. of Beit Shean, f. 1946, named for R. Naftali Tzvi Yehuda Berlin (1816–93), head of Volozhin *yeshiva*; leader in Hoveve Zion; known as "the Natziv;" father of M. Bar-Ilan**

Ein Hashofet kibbutz W. of Megiddo, f. 1938, named for Brandeis**

Ein Ibrahim village E. of Zichron Ya'akov, named for son (d. 632) of Muhammed

Einstein Albert Einstein (1879–1955), professor of physics; Nobel Prize winner (1921); humanitarian and Zionist

Eisenberg Aaron Eisenberg (1863–1931), pioneer settler in Rehovot; leader in B'ne Moshe Order

Elazari-Volcani see **Volcani**

Eliasberg R. Mordecai Eliasberg (1817–89), pioneer; leader in Hoveve Zion

Eliash Mordecai Eliash (1892–1950), Israel's 1st minister to London, 1949

Eli HaCohen see **Cohen, Eli**

Elijah Biblical prophet during reigns of Ahab and Ahaziah (9th cent. B.C.E.); destroyed prophets of Baal (I Kings 18:40), fled Jezebel (19:3), confronted Ahab (21:20)

Elijah House, St. see **Mar Elias**

Eliot George Eliot, pseudonym of Mary Anne Evans (1819–80), novelist (incl. *Daniel Deronda*)

Elisha Biblical prophet, successor to Elijah (II Kings 2:15)

Eliyahu Hanavi see **Elijah**

Eshel Avraham named for tree associated with Avraham Avinu**

Eshel Hanassi agricultural school N.W. of Beer Sheva, named for Chaim Weizmann**

Eshkol Levi Eshkol (1895–1969), leader in HaPo'el HaTza'ir, Mapai, Jewish Agency; prime minister of Israel, Knesset member, minister of finance

Esther Hamalka Queen Esther; see Biblical book of Esther

Estori HaParhi (1280–1355), 1st topographer of Eretz Israel (*Sefer Kaftor vaFerah*)

Even Sapir *moshav* W. of Jerusalem, f. 1950, named for book by R. Ya'akov HaLevi Sapir (1822–85)

Even Yehuda rural settlement near Netanya, f. 1932, named for E. Ben-Yehuda**

Ezra key figure in reconstruction of Jerusalem after the First Return from Exile; see book of Ezra

Faisal Faisal (1885–1933), king of Iraq; with Chaim Weizmann author of important agreement (1919) to implement Balfour Declaration on Jewish settlement in Palestine

Farbstein Yehoshua Heshel Farbstein (1870–1948), leader in Hoveve Zion, Mizrahi; member of Zionist Executive

Fatimiya Fatimah (606–32), daughter of Muhammed, from whom the Fatimid (Shi'ite) dynasty took its name

Feldman R. Reuven Feldman (b. 1899), General Zionist; member of Knesset

Feuerring Isaac Feuerring (1889–1937), banker, leader in General Zionism

Fischel Aaron Israel Fischel (1865–1948), American philanthropist

Fischel Institute, Jerusalem

Fishman see **Maimon**

Fleg Edmond Flegenheimer (1874–1963), French poet and playwright

Francis, St. St. Francis of Assisi (1182–1226), founder of Franciscan Order

Frank R. Zvi Pesach Frank (1873–1960), Chief Rabbi of Jerusalem

Rabbi P. Frank

Frank Sinatra International Student Centre Francis Albert Sinatra (b. 1915), popular American singer and motion picture actor ("The House I Live In," "From Here to Eternity")

Freud Sigmund Freud (1856–1939), founder of psychoanalysis; author of *Moses and Monotheism*

Friedman R. David Friedman (1812–1917), leader in Hibbat Zion (1884 Kattowitz Conference, Bilu pioneers)

Frischmann David Frischmann (1860–1922), writer and literary critic, translator

Fromchenko Eliahu Fromchenko (b. 1886), chocolate manufacturer and philanthropist

Frug Shimon Samuel Frug (1860–1916), poet in Russian and Yiddish

Fuld R. Aaron Ben Moses Fuld (1790–1847), Talmudist, leader in Frankfurt Jewish community

Fulk family name of Counts of Anjou; occasional ruling lines in Hungary, Poland, Naples, Lorraine; Foulques le Jeune, Crusader king of Jerusalem, 1131–43

Gad son of Jacob (Gen. 35:26; 49:19); "he shall overcome at the last"

Gal'ed (Even Yitzhak) kibbutz near Megiddo, f. 1945, named for Isaac Hochberg, S. African Zionist

Gamal, Mt. R. Gamaliel the Elder (*rabban*), who died c. 50 C.E.; Jewish sage, teacher of St. Paul

Gamaliel the Elder see **Gamal, Mt.**

Gan Hayim *moshav* near Kfar Sava, f. 1935, named for Chaim Weizmann**

Ganne Yohanan *moshav* near Rehovot, f. 1950, named for Johann Kremenetsky**

Gan Shlomo (Kvutzat Schiller) kibbutz W. of Rehovot, f. 1927, named for R. Solomon Mayer Schiller-Szinessy (1820–90), professor and editor of Hebrew MSS at Cambridge University

Gan Shmuel kibbutz near Hadera, f. 1913, named for R. Shmuel Mohilewer**

Gan Yoshiya *moshav* E. of Netanya, f. 1949, named for Josiah C. Wedgwood**

Gaster Moses Gaster (1856–1939), head of English Sephardim; professor at Oxford; delegate to Zionist Congresses

Gatt Ben-Zion Gatt (1909–56), teacher, historian of Jewish settlement in Palestine; leader in Haganah in Jerusalem

Gedaliyahu Gedalia, governor of Judah under the Babylonians (from 586 B.C.E.); anniversary of his death is noted in Jewish calendar (Tishri 3)

Gedud Barak Israel army battalion, named for Biblical Barak**

George Hamelech King George V, monarch of the United Kingdom (1911–36), during whose reign the Balfour Declaration was issued (1917)

Gershom R. Gershom Ben Judah Me'or HaGolah/ Rabbenu Gershom (c. 960–1028), Talmudic scholar, head of *yeshiva* in Mainz

Al-Ghazali Abu-Hamid Muhammed al-Ghazali (1058–1111), Muslim philosopher, teacher (Baghdad), mystic and monk

Gideon Biblical judge who delivered Israel from the Midianites (Judg. 6:11–8:32)

Gil'adi Israel Gil'adi (1886–1918), founder of HaShomer (1907), defence force of the Jewish colonies in the Turkish period

Gissin Ephraim Gissin (b. 1900), member of Jewish Legion in WWI; leader in Israel Farmers' Federation

Giv'at Ada village S.E. of Zichron Ya'akov, f. 1903, named for Adelaide, wife of Baron Edmond de Rothschild**

Giv'at Brenner   kibbutz near Rehovot, f. 1928, named for J.H. Brenner**

Giv'at Chaim   *kibbutzim* "A" and "B" near Netanya, f. 1952, named for Hayim Victor Arlosoroff**

Giv'at Haviva   educational institution of HaShomer Ha-Tza'ir E. of Hadera, f. 1951, named for H. Reik**

Giv'at Hen   *moshav* near Kfar Sava, f. 1933, named for Hayyim Nahman (Hen) Bialik**

Giv'at Olga   suburb of Hadera, named for Olga, wife of Y.H. Hankin**

Giv'at Shapira   *moshav* N. of Netanya, f. 1958, named for H. Schapira**

Giv'at Sha'ul   R. Ya'akov Shaul Ben Eliezer Jeroham Elyashar (1817–1906), Sephardic Chief Rabbi

Giv'at Shmuel   settlement N.E. of Tel Aviv, f. 1942, named for S. Pineles**

Giv'at Yeshiyahu   *moshav* S. of Beit Shemesh, f. 1958, named for Yeshiyahu Press (1874–1955), editor of topo-graphical-historical encyclopedia of Eretz Israel

Giv'ot Zeid   village, now a suburb of Kiriyat Tiv'on, f. 1943, named for A. Zeid**

Gluskin   Ze'ev Gluskin (1859–1949), founder of B'ne Moshe Order; a founder of Rehovot; publisher and pioneer

Gold   R. Ze'ev Gold (1889–1956), leader in Mizrahi and Jewish Agency

Goldberg   Abraham Goldberg (1883–1942), author and orator; Zionist leader in USA (American Jewish Congress, ZOA)

Goldberg   Lea Goldberg (1911–70), Hebrew poet; profes-sor at Hebrew University

Goldman   Nahum Goldman Centre, named for Nahum Goldman (b. 1895), Zionist statesman and publisher (*Encyc-lopedia Judaica*, 1925–33); president of WZO 1955–68; see Beit Hatfutzot*

N. Goldman

Goldstein   Peretz Goldstein (1923–44), parachutist captured in Italy in WWII, probably killed in KZ Oranienburg

Golomb   Eliyahu Golomb (1893–1945), pioneer of Ha-Shomer and Haganah defence organizations

Gordon   Aharon David Gordon (1856–1922), philosopher of labour; memorialized at Degania

Gordon   Judah Leib Gordon (1831–92), Hebrew poet, teacher and translator; editor of *HaMeliz*

Graetz   Heinrich (Zvi Hirsch) Graetz (1817–91), leader of German Jewry; author of *History of the Jews* (11 volumes)   119

Granott Abraham Granott (1890–1962), writer and publicist; president of Jewish National Fund; leader of Progressive Party and Knesset member; leader in Hebrew University

Grasty see **H. Graetz**

Gruenbaum Yitzhak Gruenbaum (1879–1970), writer and journalist; member of Knesset and 1st minister of the interior

Gruner Dov Gruner (1912–47), executed by British as underground fighter

Gur Yehuda (Grasowski) Gur (1862–1950), pioneer and teacher, active in B'ne Moshe Order; edited popular dictionary of Hebrew

Gutmacher R. Elijah Gutmacher (1796–1874), Talmudist, associate of R. Kalischer** in early Zionism

Ha'ari "the Lion," popular name for R. Isaac Ben Solomon Ashkenazi Luria (1534–72), Kabbalist in Safad; important for concepts of *zimzum* (hiding of the face) and *tikkun* (restitution of the right order of the universe)

Habakkuk Habakkuk (7th cent. B.C.E.), prophet of Judah; see book of Habakkuk; a commentary was found among the Dead Sea Scrolls (see Shrine of the Book*)

Hafetz Haim kibbutz E. of Ashdod, f. 1944, named for R. Israel Meir HaKohen of Radin (1835–1933), after the title of his first book; author of commentary on *Shulhan Arukh*

Hagar concubine of Abraham, mother of Ishmael (Gen. 16), mythical ancestor of Arabs

Haggai Biblical prophet (from 520 B.C.E.); see book of Haggai

Hagiz father and son, rabbis and scholarly opponents of Shabbetai Zevi: Jacob (1620–74), head of *yeshiva* in Jerusalem; Moses (1672–1751?)

Hagra R. Elijah Ben Solomon Zalman (1720–97), *gaon* of Vilna; scholar and opponent of Hasidism

Hai Ga'on R. Hai Ben Sherira (998–1038), *gaon* of Pumbedita (Babylonia); authority on *Halakha*

Hakalir Eleazar Hakalir (7th cent.), Jewish poet, resident in Tiberias

Hakim Eliahu Hakim (d. 1945), fighter against British Mandate authorities (member of Lehi), executed by the British

Halevi see **Yehuda Halevi**

Halpern Jeremiah Halpern (1901–62), pioneer in Betar, Haganah Leumit, Bergson group defence organizations; founder of Marine Museum

Hamabit acronym for R. Moses Ben Joseph Trani (1500–80), successor to R. Caro** in Safad

Hamodai R. Elazar Hamodai (2nd cent.), Talmudic scholar

Hanasi Harishon see **Weizmann**

Al-Hanawi Yakut al-Hanawi (1179–1229), Arab traveller, author of geographic dictionary

Hankin Yehoshua Hankin (1864–1945), pioneer settler and land agent

Hanna Biblical mother of the prophet Samuel (I Sam. 1:20)

Hantke Arthur Menahem Hantke (1874–1955), leader in WZO, Jewish Agency

Al-Hariri al-Kasim Ibn Ali al-Hariri (1054–1122), Muslim language scholar and writer

Harlap R. Ya'akov Moshe Harlap (1883–1951), educator and associate of R. Kook**

Hasdai Shaprut see **Ibn Shaprut**

Hatishbi Elijah the Tishbite; see Elijah**

Haviv R. Haim Haviv (1882–1942?), leader of Jewish community of Salonica (Greece)

Heftziba kibbutz W. of Beit Shean, f. 1922, named for Biblical figure (Isa. 62:4 — "Thou shalt no more be termed Forsaken; neither shall thy land any more be termed Desolate: but thou shalt be called *Hephzibah*, and thy land Beulah..."); see Beit Alfa*

Heine Heinrich Heine (1797–1856), German lyric poet ("Die Lorelei," "Du bist wie eine Blume," etc.)

Helena, St. Helena (died c. 330), mother of Emperor Constantine; pilgrim and identifier of Christian shrines

Heleni Hamalka Queen Helen of Adiabene, who in the 1st century converted to Judaism and moved to Jerusalem

Hen see **Bialik**

Herzl Theodor Herzl (1860–1904), founder of political Zionism; author of *The Jewish State*, *Old-New Land*; tomb at Mt. Herzl in Jerusalem

T. Herzl

Herzliya city N. of Tel Aviv, named for Herzl**

Herzog R. Isaac Halevi Herzog (1888–1959), Chief Rabbi of Ireland, later of Israel; leader in Mizrahi

Heshin Shneur Zalman Heshin (1903–59), Israel Supreme Court Justice

Hess Moses Hess (1812–75), pioneer socialist thinker; author of *Rome and Jerusalem*

Hildesheimer Orthodox rabbis, father and son, leaders in German Jewry: Azriel (1820–89), opposed Reform Judaism; founder of Berlin rabbinical seminary (1873); supported colonization of Palestine; Meir H. (1864–1934), director of Berlin seminary, communal leader

Hillel R. Hillel (fl. at turn of the 1st century C.E.), head of school of Beit Hillel; president of Sanhedrin   121

Hiram (c. 969–936 B.C.E.), king of Tyre, ally who helped equip Solomon's Temple

Hirsch Baron Maurice de Hirsch (1831–96), philanthropist (Alliance Israelite Universelle, Jewish Colonization Assoc.)

Baron M. de Hirsch

Hizkiyahu Hamelech King Hezekiah (727–698 B.C.E.), reformer; built tunnel, see Hezekiah's Tunnel*

Hos Dov Hos (1894–1940), a leader of Haganah; a founder of Ahdut Avoda and Histadrut

Hosea 1st of the minor prophets; see book of Hosea

Huebner Rachel Mazur Huebner, leader in Haganah and Women's Army; leader in WIZO

Hugo Victor Marie Hugo (1802–85), French poet, dramatist, novelist *(The Hunchback of Notre Dame, Les Miserables)*

Hussein Kamil Hussein (1850?–1917), sultan of Egypt

Al-Husseini Abd al-Kadar al-Husseini (d. 1948), commander of Arab forces in Jerusalem area during the War of Independence

Huysmans Camille Huysmans (1871–1968), Belgian writer, statesman and professor; executive secretary of the Labour and Socialist International Bureau in Brussels 1904–21; president of Belgian parliament and prime minister

Hyrcanus John Hyrcanus I, Hasmonean ruler 134–104 B.C.E.

Ibn Batutta Muhammed Ibn Abdullah Ibn Battuta (1304–77), Arab traveller and writer

Ibn Ezra Abraham Ben Meir Ibn Ezra (1092–1167), poet, scholar in medieval Spain; writer on many subjects, including Bible commentaries

Ibn Gabirol Solomon Ben Judah/Avicebron (1021?–1058?), Hebrew poet (incl. contributions to the liturgy); Jewish philosopher who influenced Christian scholastics

Ibn Khaldun Abd ar-Rahman Ibn Khaldun (1332–1406), Arab historian; a founder of modern sociology

Ibn Rushd Averroes/Abu al-Walid Muhammed Ibn Rushd (1126–98), Spanish-Arabian philosopher (commentary on Aristotle) who influenced Christian scholastics

Ibn Shaprut Hasdai Abu Yusuf Ibn Shaprut (915?–970), Jewish scholar and educator in medieval Spain

Ibn Sina Avicenna/Abu Ali al-Husayn Ibn Sina (980–1037), Arab physician, philosopher and writer (textbook on Aristotle that influenced Christian scholastics)

Iddo Hanavi Biblical prophet, father of Zechariah** (Ezra 5:1)

Al-Idrisi Abu Abdullah Muhammed Ibn Muhammed al-Idrisi (1100–66), Arab geographer and cartographer under King Roger II of Sicily

Imber Naftali Herz Imber (1856–1908), Hebrew poet (Barkai series), author of "HaTikva"

Isaiah Biblical prophet; see book of Isaiah; at the Shrine of the Book an important text is displayed from the Dead Sea Scrolls

Ish Gamzu Nahum of Gimzo (late 1st-early 2nd cent.), *tanna*, teacher of R. Akiva

Jabotinsky Vladimir (Ze'ev) Jąbotinsky (1880–1940), founder of Jewish Legion in WWI; pioneer of Haganah; founder of Revisionists

Jaffe Leib Jaffe (1875–1948), poet and essayist; Zionist leader; editor of *Ha'aretz*

Japheth son of Noah (Gen. 9:18)

Jaures Jean Leon Jaures (1859–1914), French socialist statesman; founder and editor of *L'Humanité*

Jeremiah Biblical prophet (7th–6th cent. B.C.E.); see book of Jeremiah

Joffe Hillel Joffe (1864–1936), physician and pioneer; leader in Hoveve Zion

Josephthal Giora Josephthal (1912–62), leader of He-Halutz in Germany, Jewish Agency, Mapai; negotiator with German Federal Republic on restitution

Joshua see **Yehoshua Bin Nun**

Julianus Julian the Apostate (331–63 C.E.), Roman ruler who permitted the rebuilding of the Temple

Kadourie School Sir Ellis Kadourie (1865–1922), commercial leader in Hong Kong and philanthropist

Al-Kais Imru al-Kais (500–540?), Arab poet of pre-Muslim period

Kalai David Kalai (b. 1898), author and publisher (Ahad Ha'am Publ., Stiebel Publ., Histadrut publications)

Kalischer R. Zvi Hirsh Kalischer (1795–1874), pioneer Zionist (Hoveve Zion)

Kaplan Eliezer Kaplan (1891–1952), a founder of Tze'ire Zion–HaPo'el HaTza'ir, Hitahadut; leader in Jewish Agency; Cabinet member

Kaplansky Shlomo Kaplansky (1884–1950), leader in Po'ale Zion, Jewish Agency; a founder of Keren HaYesod; educator, head of the Technion

Katz Benzion Katz (1907–68), Hebrew translator and educator; leader in Jewish Agency; professor and rector at Tel Aviv University

Katzir Aharon Katzir (1914–72), physicist, professor at Weizmann Institute; president of Israel Academy; killed by terrorists

Katznelson Berl Katznelson (1887–1944), philosopher of Labour movement; a founder of Histadrut, Mapai, Bank HaPo'alim; writer and editor (*Davar*)

B. Katznelson

Keller Helen Adams Keller (1880–1968), blind and deaf American author (*The Story of My Life*, 1902, *Out of the Dark*, 1910)

Kennedy Memorial, Jerusalem John F. Kennedy (1917–63), president of the USA

Kerem Ben Zimra *moshav* N. of Safad, f. 1949, named for Talmudic sages Zimra and Yossi

Kerem Maharal *moshav* on Mt. Carmel, f. 1949, named for R. Judah Liwa (Maharal) of Prague (16th cent.), reputed to have created the mythical Golem

Kever Rahel Rachel's Tomb, near Bethlehem, restored by Sir Moses Montefiore** (Gen. 35:16–20); see Rahel Imenu**

Kfar Azar *moshav* E. of Tel Aviv, f. 1932, named for Alexander Siskind Rabinowitz/Azar (1854–1945), Labour Zionist leader

Kfar Baruch *moshav* W. of Afula, f. 1926, named for Barukh Kahana, philanthropist from Romania

Kfar Bialik cooperative village near Haifa, f. 1934, named for Bialik**

Kfar Bin Nun *moshav* S.E. of Ramla, f. 1952, named for Biblical Yehoshua Bin Nun**

Kfar Blum kibbutz near Kiriyat Shmona, f. 1943, named for Leon Blum (1872–1950), socialist leader and French premier

Kfar Daniel *moshav* E. of Ramla, f. 1949, named for Daniel Frisch, president of American Zionist Federation

Kfar Gide'on *moshav* S. of Nazareth, f. 1923, named for Biblical Gideon**

Kfar Gil'adi kibbutz near Rosh Pina, f. 1916, named for I. Gil'adi**

Kfar Glickson kibbutz E. of Caesarea, f. 1939, named for Moshe Joseph Glickson (1878–1939), writer and editor (*Ha'aretz*)

Kfar Gvirol settlement W. of Rehovot, named for Ibn Gabirol**

Kfar Haim *moshav* N. of Netanya, f. 1933, named for H.V. Arlosoroff**

Kfar Hanassi kibbutz E. of Rosh Pina, f. 1948, named for C. Weizmann**

Kfar Haro'eh *moshav* near Netanya, f. 1934, named for R. Kook**; location of Bnei Akiva *yeshiva*, first of a network of *yeshivot* in Israel

Kfar Hess *moshav* N.E. of Herzliya, f. 1933, named for M. Hess**

Kfar Kisch *moshav* E. of Nazareth, f. 1946, named for Lt. Col. Kisch**

Kfar Maimon *moshav* S.E. of Gaza, f. 1959, named for R. Maimon**

Kfar Malal *moshav* N. of Petah Tikva, f. 1922; see Lilienblum**

Kfar Masaryk kibbutz near Haifa, f. 1938, named for T. Masaryk**

Kfar Menahem kibbutz W. of Beit Shemesh, f. 1939, named for M.M. Ussishkin**

Kfar Monash *moshav* E. of Netanya, f. 1946; see Monash**

Kfar Mordechai *moshav* N.E. of Ashdod, f. 1950, named for M. Eliash**

Kfar Nahum see **Capernaum***

Kfar Netter *moshav* S. of Netanya, f. 1939; see Netter**

Kfar Pines *moshav* N.E. of Hadera, f. 1933; see Pines**

Kfar Ruppin kibbutz near Beit Shean, f. 1938, named for A. Ruppin**

Kfar Shammai *moshav* near Safad, f. 1949, named for R. Shammai**

Kfar Shmariyahu *moshav* near Herzliya, f. 1937, named for S. Levin**; its communal hall was built by Sir Arthur Grenfell Wauchope (1874–1947), High Commissioner for Palestine 1931–38

Kfar Shmuel *moshav* S.E. of Ramla, f. 1950, named for S. Wise**

Kfar Silver agricultural school near Ashkelon, f. 1957; see Silver**

Kfar Syrkin *moshav* E. of Petah Tikva, f. 1936, named for N. Syrkin**

Kfar Szold kibbutz near Kiriyat Shmona, f. 1942, named for H. Szold**

Kfar Truman *moshav* E. of Lod, f. 1949, named for Harry S. Truman**

Kfar Warburg *moshav* S.E. of Ashdod, f. 1939, named for Felix M. Warburg (1871–1937), American financier and philanthropist

Kfar Vitkin *moshav* N. of Netanya, f. 1933, named for Y. Vitkin**

Kfar Yabetz *moshav* E. of Netanya, f. 1932, named for Ze'ev Jawitz (1847–1924), Hebrew author and educator; religious Zionist philosopher (Mizrahi)

Kfar Yehezkiel *moshav* S.E. of Afula, f. 1921, named for Sir Ezekiel Sassoon (1860–1932), Iraqi-Jewish statesman

Kfar Yehoshua *moshav* S.E. of Kiriyat Tiv'on, f. 1927, named for Y. Hankin**

Khaled Ibn al-Walid (d. 642), Arab general who conquered Syria, defeated Byzantium, won battle of the Yarmuk (636)

Al-Khalidiye Ruhi al-Khalidiye (1864–1914), Arab scholar

Al-Khalil "the Friend" — Arab name for Abraham, patriarch, and for Hebron; see Avraham Avinu**

Al-Khattab Omar Ibn al-Khattab (581?–644), "Emperor of Believers;" conqueror of Syria, Palestine, Egypt; introduced Muslim system of dating from the *Hegira* (622 C.E.)

Khoushi Abba Khoushi (Hushi, Schneller: 1898–1969), a founder of Beit Alfa; leader in building Haifa harbour, in Histadrut, Haganah; mayor of Haifa

Kimchi see **Radak**

Kiriyat Bialik see **Bialik**

Kiriyat Eliyahu see **Elijah**

Kiriyat Hayim see **Arlosoroff**

Kiriyat Moshe see **Montefiore**

Kiriyat Motzkin see **Motzkin**

Kiriyat Shmuel suburb of Haifa, named for Shmuel Hayyim Landau (1892–1928), leader of Young Mizrahi; coined *Tora va Avoda* (Torah and Labour)

Kisch Frederick Herman Kisch (1888–1943), British career officer; served with Weizmann in Zionist Executive and Jewish Agency; a builder of Haifa (incl. Technion)

Klausner Josef Gedalia Klausner (1874–1958), Zionist leader; editor (*Betar, HaShilo'ah, Encyclopedia Hebraica*); prolific scholarly writer (incl. *Jesus of Nazareth, History of Modern Hebrew Literature*)

Klein Samuel Klein (1886–1940), historian and geographer; taught at Hebrew University

Klutznick B'nei B'rith Library, Jerusalem Philip M. Klutznick (b. 1907), American public and communal leader; co-founder of modern Ashdod

König Pierre König (b. 1898), French general in WWII; chairman of French Friends of Israel

Kook R. Abraham Isaac Kook (1865–1935), scholar and Zionist (Mizrahi, Agudat Israel); founder of Jerusalem *yeshiva* Merkaz HaRav; Chief Rabbi of Palestine

Rabbi A. Kook

Kook Foundation Jerusalem centre of World Mizrahi movement, with extensive cultural, research and publishing activities; named for R. Kook**

Korczak Janusz Korczak (1878–1942), Polish Jew, educator and martyr; memorialized also at Yad Vashem

Koresh Cyrus the Great (600?–529 B.C.E.), king of Persia, sponsor of the First Return from Exile

Kossovsky R. Haim Joshua Kossovsky (1873–1960), Talmudist, author of Mishnah concordance

Kremenetsky Johann Kremenetsky (1850–1934), engineer and inventor; friend of Herzl** and organizer of Jewish National Fund

Krinitzi Abraham Krinitzi (1886–1969), leader in Po'ale Zion; pioneer industrialist and manufacturer; leader in Tel Aviv and Ramat Gan governments; a founder of Bar–Ilan University**

LaGuardia Fiorella LaGuardia (1882–1947), member U.S. House of Representatives (1917–21, 1923–33); mayor of New York City (1934–45)

Lahavot Haviva kibbutz E. of Hadera, f. 1949, named for H. Reik**

Lampronti R. Isaac Hezekiah Ben Samuel Lampronti (1679–1756), Italian head of *yeshiva*; author of many-volumed *halakhic* survey

Leah wife of Biblical patriarch Jacob (Gen. 29:23–26)

Lefrak Garden, Jerusalem Samuel J. Lefrak (b. 1918), U.S. builder and philanthropist

Levi Shabbetai Levi (1876–1956), a founder of the Technion; mayor of Haifa

Levin R. Isaac Meir Levin (b. 1893), leader in Agudat Israel; member of Knesset and Cabinet

Levin Shmarya Levin (1867–1935), editor and writer; active in Zionist Congresses; a founder of the Technion, Dvir Publ. House, Keren HaYesod

Levinsky Yom Tov Levinsky (b. 1899), leader of Jewish Folklore Society; editor Dvir Publ. House

Levontin Zalman David Levontin (1856–1940), active in Hoveve Zion; a founder of Rishon Letzion, Bank Leumi

Liessin pseudonym of Abraham Walt (1872–1938), Yiddish poet, translator and editor

Lilienblum Moshe Leib Lilienblum (1843–1910), Hebrew and Yiddish writer in Russia; leader in Hoveve Zion; associate of J.L. Gordon** and L. Pinsker**

Liman *moshav* N. of Nahariya, f. 1949, named for Herbert H. Lehman (1878–1963), American banker and statesman, a founder of American Jewish Joint Distribution Committee (1941)

Lincoln Abraham Lincoln (1809–65), president of the USA, "the Great Emancipator"

A. Lincoln

Luncz Abraham Moses Luncz (1854–1918), author and editor (almanac: *Lu'ah Eretz Israel*)

Luz Kaddish (Luzinsky) Luz (b. 1895), leader in Histadrut, Mapai; member of Knesset and Cabinet

Ma'agan Michael kibbutz N. of Caesarea, f. 1949, named for Michael Pollack of PICA

Ma'ayan Baruch kibbutz near Kiriyat Shmona, f. 1947, named for Baruch Gordon, S. African Zionist

Ma'ayan Tzevi kibbutz N.E. of Caesarea, f. 1938, named for Harry (Tzevi) Frank of PICA

Maccabim family of the Maccabees, more correctly Hasmoneans, who raised the revolt (167 B.C.E.) against paganism, defeated the Syrians, and ruled the Jewish nation to 63 B.C.E.

Machnes Gad Machnes (b. 1899), pioneer in citrus industry; director of many marketing agencies

Magnes R. Judah Leon Magnes (1877–1948), educator and statesman; head of Hebrew University 1925–48

Mahane Yisrael Township N. of Ramla, f. 1950, named for Yisrael Shehori (d. 1948), Haganah officer killed in the War of Independence

Maimon R. Judah Leib Fishman (1876–1962), leader in Mizrahi; writer and communal leader; his sister Ada (b. 1893) was also an outstanding leader (WZO, Histadrut, Mapai, WIZO) and writer

Maimonides see **Rambam**

Makor Baruch sector of Jerusalem, f. 1924, named for Baruch Hershenoff

Malachi Biblical prophet (fl. 464–24 B.C.E.); see book of Malachi

Malal see **Lilienblum**

Malkitzedek Biblical Melchizedek, king of Salem (Jerusalem) (Gen. 14:18–20)

Al-Ma'mun Abu al-Abbas Abdullah al-Ma'mun (786–833), 7th caliph of Baghdad, patron of astronomy and philosophy

Mani R. Elijah Ben Suleiman Mani (1818–99), Chief Rabbi of Hebron 1865–99

Mann Frederick R. Mann (b. 1903), U.S. diplomat and philanthropist

Ma'oz Haim kibbutz near Beit Shean, f. 1937; see Sturman**

Al-Maqdisi Muhammed Ibn Ahmad al-Maqdisi (c. 946–c. 996), Arab geographer and author

Marcus David Marcus (1902–48), American officer who served in WWII and occupation of Germany; killed while commander of defence of Jerusalem in War of Independence

D. Marcus

Mar Elias Greek Orthodox monastery (6th cent.) on Jerusalem-Bethlehem road (I Kings 19:3)

Margaliyot *moshav* near Kiriyat Shmona, f. 1951, named for R. Reuben Margaliot (1889–1971), scholar, author and editor; received Israel Prize 1957

Mar Saba Greek Orthodox monastery f. 483, named for St. Saba (493–532); see Karantal*

Masaryk Thomas Masaryk (1850–1937), political philosopher and statesman; 1st president of Czechoslovakia

Mash'abei Sadeh kibbutz in the Negev S. of Beer Sheva, f. 1949, named for Y. Sadeh**

Mazkeret Batya village S.E. of Rehovot, f. 1883 as Ekron; renamed 1948 for mother of Baron Edmond de Rothschild**

Mass Dani Mass (d. 1948), commander in the Palmach, killed in Gush Etzion action

Massuot Yitzhak *moshav* N. of Tel Aviv, f. 1949, named for R. Herzog**

Matitiyahu Mattathias/Matthew (d. 167 B.C.E.), leader of revolt against the Syrians (Seleucids) that founded the Hasmonean kingdom and dynasty

Matzliach *moshav* S. of Ramla, f. 1950, named for Sahel Ben Matzliah (10th cent.), Karaite scholar and writer

Meir R. Ya'akov Akhva Meir (1856–1939), leader in Salonica, then Chief Rabbi of Palestine (Sephardic)

Meir Forest, near Hebron see **Bar-Ilan**

Melchett see **Mond**

Menahemiya *moshav* S. of Kinneret, f. 1902 by PICA, after WWI named for Menahem, the father of Sir Herbert Samuel**

Mendele Mocher Sefarim ("Mendele the Book-seller") pseudonym of Shalom Jacob Abramovitsch (1835–1917), Hebrew and Yiddish writer

Mendelssohn Moses Mendelssohn (1729–86), philosopher of German Enlightenment; friend of Lessing ("Nathan der Weise"); author of *Jerusalem*

Metzudat Yesha ruins N. of Safad with a Muslim tomb memorializing Yehoshua Bin Nun**

Metzudot Ussishkin a cluster of settlements near Kiriyat Shmona, named for M.M. Ussishkin**

Meyuhas Yosef Baran Meyuhas (1868–1942), leader of the Sephardic community in Eretz Israel, writer and educator

Micah prophet in Judah (8th cent. B.C.E.); see book of Micah

Michael angel viewed as defender of the Jewish people (Daniel 12:1)

Michal daughter of King Saul and wife of King David (I Sam. 14:49; II Sam. 3:14)

Midrashat Ruppin agricultural school near Netanya, named for A. Ruppin**

Mintz Binyamin Mintz (1903–61), leader in Agudat Israel; member of Knesset and Cabinet

Miriam Mary, mother of Jesus (Matt. 1:16)

Miriam Hanevia Miriam, the prophetess, sister of Moses (Ex. 15:20–21; Micah 6:4)

Misgav Dov *moshav* E. of Ashdod, f. 1950, named for Dov Gruner**

Mishmar David kibbutz E. of Rehovot, f. 1948, named for David Marcus**

Mitudela see **Binyamin Mitudela**

Mivtzar Nimrod Nimrod, mighty hunter (Gen. 10:9); see Yehi'am*

Mohilewer R. Shmuel Mohilewer (1824–98), writer and teacher; founder of Hoveve Zion; member of Zionist Congress Executive

Molcho R. Solomon Molcho (c. 1500–32), Marrano, Kabbalist, messianic preacher

Monash Sir John Monash (1865–1931), Australian general in WWI; vice-chancellor of Melbourne University

Mond British family: Alfred Moritz (1868–1930), 1st Baron Melchett, member of Parliament and Cabinet; a founder of Jewish Agency; Henry M. (1898–1949), chairman of Jewish Agency Council

Montefiore Sir Moses Montefiore (1784–1885), financier and philanthropist; founder of Mishkenot Sha'ananim quarter outside the Old City, and many agricultural settlements and schools

Sir Moses Montefiore

Moshe Rabenu "Moses our Teacher" (13th cent. B.C.E.), prophet and leader of the Exodus; lawgiver at Sinai (10 Commandments); see Biblical Pentateuch

Motzkin Leo (Arye Leib) Motzkin (1867–1933), a founder of WZO; co-author of Basel Programme

Mukhtar Ahmed Mukhtar Pasha (1832–1919), Turkish general and colonial administrator

Murray Centre, Eilat Philip Murray (1886–1952), American labour leader; president of the CIO

Naftali Naphtali, son of Jacob (Gen. 49:21; Deut. 33:23)

Nahalat Jabotinsky settlement N.E. of Caesarea, named for Jabotinsky**

Nahalat Shimon sector of Jerusalem, named for Simon the Just**

Nahalat Yehuda *moshav* near Rishon Letzion, f. 1914, named for Y. Pinsker**

Nahalat Zadok Jerusalem suburb, f. 1908, named for French Chief Rabbi Zadok HaCohen

Nahmanides see **Ramban**

Nahshon Biblical Nahshon, son of Amminadab (Num. 1:7), captain of army of Judah (Num. 2:3)

Nahum prophet; see book of Nahum, composed shortly after fall of Ninevah (612 B.C.E.)

Najara Israel Ben Moses Najara (1530?–99?), Hebrew poet and liturgist

Naomi   Bible figure; see book of Ruth

Narkiss   Mordechai Narkiss (1898–1957), curator and art historian; manager of Bezalel School of Art

An-Nasser   Gamal Abdel Nasser (1918–70), president of Egypt

Nathan   Isaac Nathan (1790?–1864), composer, including setting Byron's *Hebrew Melodies* to music

Nathan Hanavi   Biblical prophet in time of David and Solomon (I Chron. 17:1–15; II Sam. 12:1–15; I Kings 1:32–45)

Nathanson   R. Joseph Saul Nathanson (1810–75), rabbi of Lemberg, opponent of Reform and Hasidism; wrote on Talmud, Maimonides

Natronai Ga'on   Natronai Bar-Hilai (9th cent.), *gaon* of Sura 853–58; opponent of the Karaites, defender of *midrashic* development

Navon   Joseph Navon (1858–1934), development pioneer in Eretz Israel (i.e. Jaffa-Jerusalem railroad)

Nebi Musa   Muslim shrine near Jericho, "Tomb of Moses"

Nebi Samwil   traditional shrine ("Tomb of Samuel") N.E. of Jerusalem, with tomb and mosque (I Sam. 25:1)

Nehemiah   rebuilder of Jerusalem, governor of Judah (5th cent. B.C.E.); see book of Nehemiah

Nehemiah   disciple of R. Akiva (2nd cent.), active in renewal of Torah teaching

Neot Mordechai   kibbutz S. of Kiriyat Shmona, f. 1946, named for Mordechai Rossovsky, Zionist leader from Argentina

Netanya   city between Tel Aviv and Haifa, named for Nathan Straus**

Netter   Charles Netter (1826–82), a founder of Alliance Israelite Universelle; established Mikveh Yisrael agricultural school

C. Netter

Netzer Sereni   kibbutz S.W. of Ramla, f. 1948, named for Enzo Sereni**

Neveh Efraim   community S.W. of Petah Tikva, f. 1953, named for Fred (Efraim) Monosson, American Jewish philanthropist

Neveh Granott   see **Granott**

Neveh Yehoshua   see **Yehoshua Bin Nun**

Necanor   Necanor of Alexandria, who donated brass doors for the Second Temple in Herod's time

Nir Akiva   *moshav* E. of Gaza, f. 1953, named for Akiba Jacob Ettinger (1872–1945), agronomist and planner of agricultural settlements in Palestine; leader in Jewish National Fund

131

Nir David kibbutz near Beit Shean, f. 1936, named for David Wolfsson**

Nir Eliyahu kibbutz E. of Herzliya, f. 1950, named for E. Golomb**

Nir Moshe *moshav* E. of Gaza, f. 1953, named for M. Smilansky**

Nir Tzevi *moshav* N.E. of Ramla, f. 1954, named for Baron (Tzevi) de Hirsch**

Nir Yaffe *moshav* S. of Afula, f. 1956, named for Mark Jaffe, S. African philanthropist

Nir Yisrael *moshav* N.E. of Ashkelon, f. 1949, named for I. Taiber**

Nir Yitzhak kibbutz in the Negev, S. of Gaza, f. 1949, named for Y. Sadeh**

Nissenbaum R. Isaac Nissenbaum (1868–1942), leader in Hoveve Zion, Mizrahi; preacher, author, editor; died in Warsaw ghetto

Noah Mordecai Manuel Noah (1785–1851), U.S. journalist, judge and politician; promoted the idea of a Jewish state in Palestine

Nordau Max Nordau, pseudonym of Simon Maximilian Suedfeld (1849–1923), leader in Zionist Congresses and historian; drafted Basel Programme (1897)

M. Nordau

Nordiya *moshav* near Netanya, f. 1948, named for Max Nordau**

Nurock R. Mordekhai Nurock (1884–1962), Mizrahi leader; leader in Zionist Congresses; member of Knesset and Cabinet

Obadiah MiBertinoro R. Obadiah Ben Abraham Yare Bertinoro (c. 1450–before 1516), traveller and writer; leader in Hebron and Jerusalem

Oded Biblical prophet (II Chron. 15:1)

Ohali'av Biblical Aholiab, appointed with Bezalel** to build Tent of Meeting (Ex. 35:30–35)

Ohel Moshe see **Montefiore**

Oliphant Laurence Oliphant (1829–88), Christian pro-Zionist and mystic

Omar Ibn al-Khattab see **Al-Khattab**

Omar Khayyam (d. c. 1123), Persian poet and astronomer; author of the *Rubaiyat*

Or Akiva township N. of Hadera, f. 1951, named for R. Akiva**

Orson Hyde Memorial Park named for the leader of the first (1846) delegation of the Church of Jesus Christ of Latterday Saints ("Mormons") to the Holy Land

Oved Biblical Obed, grandfather of King David** (Ruth 4:17)

Paley Centre Wm. S. Paley (b. 1901), U.S. radio and TV executive, chairman of CBS (1946–)

Pardess Hanna village E. of Hadera, noted for *yeshiva* high school — "the Midrashia;" named for daughter of Baron Mayer Nathan Rothschild of London

Patt Ya'akov Patt (1894–1956), in the Jewish Brigade, WWI; later Haganah commander in Jerusalem

Paulus VI Paul VI/Giovanni Battista Montini (1897–1978), who visited Israel in 1964

Pelleg Frank Pelleg (1910–68), Israel musician (piano and harpsichord)

Peretz Isaac Leib Peretz (1852–1915), Yiddish and Hebrew author

Pestalozzi Johann Heinrich Pestalozzi (1746–1827), Swiss educational pioneer and writer

Peter, St. Simon Peter (d. 67?), disciple of Jesus; according to the Roman Catholic Church, the first pope

Pethahiah Pethahiah of Regensburg, 12th century Jewish traveller, author of *Sivuv* ("Circuit")

Pevsner Samuel Joseph Pevsner (1878–1930), early Zionist, engineer, and leader in Haifa

Pineles Samuel Pineles (1843–1928), leader in Hoveve Zion; associate of Herzl** in Zionist Congresses

Pines Yehiel Michael Pines (1843–1913), Zionist philosopher; supporter of Bilu pioneers; associated with Ben-Yehuda** in revival of Hebrew

Pinkas David Zvi Pinkas (1895–1952), leader in Mizrahi; Knesset and Cabinet member

Pinsker Leo Pinsker (1821–91), writer and editor, leader in Hoveve Zion; author of *Auto-Emancipation* (1882)

L. Pinsker

Pinski David Pinski (1872–1959), Yiddish poet, playwright and editor; a leader in Po'ale Zion

Plumer Herbert Onslow Plumer (1857–1932), British Field Marshal; High Commissioner for Palestine, 1925–28

Pnina Biblical Peninnah (I Sam. 1:2,4)

Polonsky R. Simeon Polonsky (d. 1948), a founder of Beit Israel sector in Jerusalem

Rabad R. Abraham Ben David Halevi (c. 1100–80), Spanish scholar, historian and philosopher (*Emunah Ramah*)

Rabinowitz Aaron Rabinowitz (1901–45), secretary of Jewish Labour Council

Rachel's Tomb   see **Kever Rahel**

Radak   popular name of R. David Kimchi (1160?–1235?), grammarian and exegete in the Provencal, who influenced Christian scholastics; associate of Rambam**

Radek   Karl Radek (1885–1939?), Marxist revolutionary and political leader; associate of Lenin, liquidated by Stalin

Radler-Feldman   see **Binyamin Rabbi**

Rahel   pseudonym of Rahel Bluwstein (1890–1931), Hebrew poet ("Kinneret")

Rahel Imenu   "Rachel our Mother," wife of Jacob (Gen. 29:15–30), mother of Joseph (Gen. 30:22–25)

Ralbag   popular name of R. Levi Ben Gershom/ Gersonides (1288–1344), astronomer, philosopher and Biblical commentator

Ramat David   kibbutz W. of Nazareth, f. 1926, named for David Lloyd George (1863–1945), British prime minister when Balfour Declaration was issued (1917)

Ramat Hanadiv   public park near Zichron Ya'akov, burial place of Baron Edmond de Rothschild** and his wife Adelaide

Ramat Hashofet   kibbutz W. of Afula, f. 1941, named for Judge Julian Mack (1866–1943), American jurist; a founder of American Jewish Committee; leader in ZOA (Mack-Brandeis group), American Jewish Congress, UJA

Ramat Hatishbi   section of Haifa; see Elijah**

Ramat Pinkas   *moshav* near Tel Aviv, f. 1952, named for D. Pinkas**

Ramat Rahel   kibbutz on S. outskirts of Jerusalem, f. 1926; see Rahel Imenu**

Ramat Raziel   *moshav* near Jerusalem, f. 1948, named for D. Raziel**

Ramat Tzevi   *moshav* E. of Afula, f. 1942, named for Henry (Tzevi) Monsky (1890–1947), leader in American B'nei B'rith; a founder of National Community Relations Advisory Council (1944)

Ramat Yohanan   kibbutz E. of Haifa, f. 1932, named for Jan Christiaan Smuts (1870–1950), S. African prime minister and Christian supporter of Zionism

Rambam   popular name of R. Moses Maimonides (1135–1204), Jewish philosopher; author of *A Guide for the Perplexed* and *The Mishneh Torah*

Rambam

Ramban   popular name of R. Moses Ben Nahman/ Nahmanides (1194–1270), scholar; a leader in the 1263 Disputation with Christians, he had to leave Spain for Akko; buried in Jerusalem

Ramot Shapira educational centre bordering *moshav* Beit Meir** named for R. Shapira**

Ranak popular name of R. Nachman Krochmal (1785–1840), leader in the *Haskalah* (Enlightenment), pioneer in applying the historical method to *Halakha* and *Aggada*

Rappoport R. Baruch Rappoport (d. 1946), a founder of sector Beit Israel in Jerusalem

Ras ad-Din Rashid ad-Din (1250?–1318), physician and historian (*History of the Mongols of Persia*)

Rashbam R. Samuel Ben Meir (c. 1080–c. 1174), bibliographer and Talmudic commentator

Rashi R. Solomon Ben Isaac (1040–1105), commentator on the Pentateuch and Babylonian Talmud

Ar-Rashid Harun ar-Rashid (764?–809), 5th caliph of Baghdad; outstanding warrior, patron of culture and diplomat (relations with Charlemagne and T'ang Dynasty of China)

Rav Eshlag see **Ashlag**

Rav Hen R. Zerahiah Ben Isaac Ben Shealtiel Gracian (13th cent.), Bible commentator and translator (Arabic into Hebrew)

Rav Tza'ir R. Haim Chernowitz (1871–1949), Talmudist; founder of modern *yeshiva* in Jerusalem

Raziel David Raziel (1910–41), commander in Irgun; killed in Baghdad on mission to counteract pro-Axis revolt of Rashid Ali

D. Raziel

Reich Leon Reich (1879–1929), Zionist leader in Poland

Reichman R. Joshua Meir Reichman (1862–1942), Ashkenazi communal leader in Jerusalem

Reik Haviva Reik (1914–44), parachutist captured and killed in Slovakia in WWII

Reines R. Isaac Jacob Reines (1839–1915), writer on *Halakha* and *Aggada*; founder of Mizrahi movement (1902)

Remez Moshe David Remez (1886–1951), a founder of Ahdut Avoda and Histadrut; chairman of Va'ad Leumi; member of Knesset and Cabinet

Reuven Reuben, a son of Jacob (Gen. 29:32)

Ridbaz R. Jacob David Ben Ze'ev Willowski (1845–1913), active in Lithuania, Chicago and Eretz Israel; founder of *yeshiva* in Safad (1905)

Rina Nikova Centre, Jerusalem named for Rina Nikova (b. 1898), Israeli dancer and choreographer

Ringelblum Dr. Emanuel Ringelblum (1900–44), historian of the Warsaw ghetto and martyr

135

Rivka Rebekah, wife of Isaac (Gen. 24:15–67; 25:20); buried at Machpela Cave, Hebron

Rivlin Yosef Yitzhak Rivlin (1837–96), writer, leader of Ashkenazi community in Jerusalem

Rockefeller Museum John D. Rockefeller, Jr. (1874–1960), American financier and philanthropist

Rokach Shimon Rokach (1863–1922), leader in the Palestinian Sephardic community

Rokah Israel Rokah (1896–1959), leader in General Zionists; mayor of Tel Aviv; member of Knesset and Cabinet

Rosanes Solomon Abraham Rosanes (1862–1938), author of major history of Jews in Turkey and the Orient

De Rothschild family of Jewish philanthropists: Edmond-James (1845–1934), "Father of the Yishuv;" James Armand (1878–1957), head of PICA, whose widow, Dorothy Pinto de R., donated money for the Knesset building; Bethsabee (b. 1914) founder of Batsheva Dance Co. in Tel Aviv

Baron E. de Rothschild

Ruppin Arthur Ruppin (1876–1943), leader in WZO, Zionist Executive; writer, professor, and planner of agricultural development

Ruth see Biblical book of Ruth

Sa'adia Ga'on Saadiah Ben Joseph (882–942), *gaon* of Babylonian Jewry; established present calendar; philosopher, grammarian and Bible commentator

Sacher Park, Jerusalem named for Harry Sacher (1881–1971), journalist (*Manchester Guardian*); Zionist Executive 1927–31; his wife Miriam a leader in WIZO; his son Michael (b. 1919) in Jewish Agency Executive

Sadeh Yitzhak Sadeh (1890–1952), a founder of HaPo'el sports organization; founder of Palmach (1941); leader in Mapam

As-Safa Ikhwan as-Safa, founder (983) of society of Arab scholars and philosophers

St. George monastery in Wadi Kilt (5th cent.), named for St. George of Coziba; see Karantal*

St. Theodosius monastery near Bethlehem, f. 476 by St. Theodosius (424–529), see Karantal*

Salah ad-Din Salah ad-Din Yusuf Ibn Ayyub (1138–93), sultan of Egypt and Syria; commander against the Crusaders, capturing Akko, Jerusalem, Ashkelon, etc.

Salant R. Samuel Salant (1816–1909), Chief Rabbi of Jerusalem; founder of *yeshiva* Etz Hayyim, Bikkur Holim Hospital

Salomon Joel Moshe Salomon (1838–1912), pioneer settler, writer and editor; a founder of Petah Tikva

Samuel Sir Herbert Louis Samuel (1870–1963), British statesman; 1st British High Commissioner for Palestine

Samuel Ben Adia (6th cent.), Jewish poet who wrote in Arabic in Arabian peninsula before rise of Islam

San Martin Jose de San Martin (1778–1850), liberator of Argentina, Chile, Peru; statesman

Sapir Joseph Sapir (1869–1935), editor and essayist; a leader in General Zionism

Schachel see **Shahal**

Schapira Hermann (Zevi Hirsch) Schapira (1840–98), mathematician; leader of Zionist movement; originator of Jewish National Fund

Schneller Ludwig Schneller (1820–96), German Protestant who set up an orphanage in Jerusalem, now serving as army base called Schneller camp

Schocken Institute library and cultural centre (poetry, mysticism), founded by Salman Schocken (1877–1959) in Germany and moved to Jerusalem in 1934

Schorr R. Moses Schorr (1874–1941), Polish scholar and communal leader

Schwarz R. Yehoseph Schwarz (1804–65), author of pioneer work on topography of Eretz Israel: *A Descriptive Geography and Brief Historical Sketch of Palestine*

Sde David *moshav* S.E. of Ashkelon, f. 1955, named for Z.D. Levontin**

Sde Eliahu kibbutz S. of Beit Shean, f. 1939, named for R. Gutmacher**

Sde Nahum kibbutz N.E. of Beit Shean, f. 1937, named for N. Sokolov**

Sde Nehemia kibbutz E. of Rosh Pina, f. 1940, named for Nehemia De Lieme (1882–1940), leader in Dutch Zionist Federation and WZO

Sde Warburg *moshav* N.E. of Herzliya, f. 1938, named for Otto Warburg**

Sde Ya'akov *moshav* near Kiriyat Tiv'on, f. 1927, named for R. Reines**

Sde Yitzhak *moshav* E. of Hadera, f. 1952, named for Y. Sadeh**

Sde Yoav kibbutz E. of Ashkelon, f. 1956, named for Isaac Dubnow (d. 1948), known as "Yoav" in the underground, killed defending kibbutz Negba

Sdot Micha *moshav* W. of Beit Shemesh, f. 1955, named for M. Bin-Gorion**

Sereni Enzo Hayim Sereni (1905–44), a founder of kibbutz Giv'at Brenner; emissary of the Jewish Agency; parachutist captured in Italy and killed in Dachau

Shabazi Shalem Shabazi (17th cent.), Yemenite Jewish poet; his tomb in Taiz became a shrine of Jews and Muslims

Shadmot Devora *moshav* E. of Nazareth, f. 1939, named for Dorothy (Devora) de Rothschild**

Shahal R. Shmuel Hayim Landau (1892–1928), leader and philosopher of HaPo'el HaMizrahi; executive of Zionist Congress and *Tora va Avoda*

Shahar Haim Dov Shahar (1891–1930), teacher and author; a founder of Beit Hakerem sector of Jerusalem

Shalag Samuel Leib Gordon (1865–1933), Hebrew poet and educator

Shalom Yehuda Avram Shalom Yehuda (1877–1951), writer, Orientalist, and Bible commentator

Shamgar deliverer of Israel in the time of the Judges (Judg. 3:31; 5:6)

Shammai Shammai the Elder (c. 50 B.C.E.–30 C.E.), leader of the Sanhedrin; founder of *halakhic* school

Shapira R. Meir Shapira (1887–1934), communal leader in Poland; founded *dat yomi* (daily Talmudic reading); founder of *yeshiva* at Lublin

Shapira (Hayim) Moshe Shapira (1902–70), leader in Mizrahi, Tora vaAvoda; executive in the Jewish Agency, member of Knesset and Cabinet

Shaprut see **Ibn Shaprut**

Sharabi R. Shalom Sharabi (1720–77), Jerusalem Kabbalist, a founder and head of "Beit El" *yeshiva*

Sharett Moshe (Shertok) Sharett (1894–1965), executive of Ahdut Avoda, Po'ale Zion; leader in Histadrut, Jewish Agency, Zionist Executive, Haganah; member of Knesset, prime minister 1953–56

M. Sharett

Sha'ul Hamelech Saul, king of Israel (ruled c. 1029–1005 B.C.E.) (I Sam. 9–10:15)

Sheikh Jarrah a 12th century warrior vs. Crusaders; sector of E. Jerusalem

Sheinkin R. Menahem Sheinkin (1871–1924), active in Hoveve Zion, early Zionist Congresses; a founder of Tel Aviv

Shekhunat Borochov sector of Tel Aviv, named for D.B. Borochov**

Shenhar Yitzhak Shenhar (1902–57), Hebrew writer and translator

Sherira Ga'on Sherira Ben Hanina (c. 906–1006), *gaon* of Pumbedita 968–1006; leader of the last flowering of the Babylonian academy (Baghdad)

Shimon Biblical Simeon, son of Jacob (Gen. 35:23)

Shimon R. Simeon bar Yohai (2nd cent.), writer of the Mishnah; *Zohar* attributed to him; buried at Meiron with son Eliezer

Shimon Hatzadik see **Simon the Just**

Shimoni David Shimoni (1886–1956), Hebrew poet and writer

Shimshon Samson, judge in Israel and enemy of the Philistines (Judg. 13–16)

Shlomo Solomon (10th cent. B.C.E.), king of Israel; builder of the Temple

Shlomo Ben Yosef Shlomo Ben Yosef (1913–38), first Jew to be executed by the British in Palestine

Shlomo Hamelech see **Shlomo**

Shlonsky Abraham Shlonsky (1900–73), Hebrew poet, editor and translator; writer for *Al HaMishmar*

Shmarya Biblical Shemariah, warrior who joined David at Ziklag (I Chron. 12:5)

Shmuel Samuel (11th cent. B.C.E.), judge and prophet (I Sam. 1:16)

Shmuel Ben Adiya see **Samuel Ben Adia**

Shmuel Hanagid Samuel HaNagid (Ibn Nagrol'a: 993–1055), poet, *halakhist*, military commander in Granada

Shmuel Hanavi see **Shmuel**

Shneur Zalman Shneur (1887–1959), Hebrew and Yiddish poet and novelist

Shneur R. Zalman Shneur of Lyady (1745–1813), Lubavitcher, founded Habad Hasidism; scholar of Talmud and Kabbala

Shnirer Sarah Shnirer (1883–1935), educator, founder of "Beit Ya'akov"

Shofman Gershon Shofman (1880–1972), Hebrew writer of short stories and essays

Sholal Isaac HaKohen Sholal (d. 1524), Talmudist, last Egyptian *nagid* under the Mamelukes

Sholom Aleichem pseudonym of Shalom Rabinowitz (1859–1916), Yiddish story writer and Zionist essayist

Shoshana Shoshana Poliakov (d. 1917), philanthropist who set up fund for religious institutions in Jerusalem

Shrira Ga'on see **Sherira Ga'on**

Shunamit the Shunammite maiden, nurse to King David (I Kings 1:3)

Silberman Alexander Silberman Institute of Life Sciences, Hebrew University, named for Alexander Silberman (b. 1901), Philadelphia industrialist and philanthropist

Silver R. Abba Hillel Silver (1893–1963), writer and orator; leader of The Temple (Cleveland, Ohio); Zionist leader (ZOA, WZO), favoured political activism

Simhoni Assaf Simhoni (1922–56), commander in Sinai campaign

Simon the Just High Priest of Jerusalem, reputed to have saved the city from pillage by Alexander the Great (332 B.C.E.)

Smilansky Moshe Smilansky (1874–1953), writer and editor; a founder of Hitahadut

Smuts see **Ramat Yohanan**

Sokolov Nahum Sokolov (1859–1936), Hebrew author (*History of Zionism*) and editor (*HaTzefira, HeAsif, Sefer HaShana, HaOlam, Die Welt*); leader in WZO

Sokolov House HQ of Israel Journalists Association, in Tel Aviv; see Sokolov**

Sonnabend Yehezkel (Henry) Sonnabend, first mayor of Ashkelon

Sonnenfeld R. Joseph Hayyim Ben Abraham Sonnenfeld (1849–1932), separatist Orthodox leader, opponent of Zionism

Sorotzkin R. Zalman Ben Ben-Zion Sorotzkin (1881–1966), leader of Agudat Israel in Poland; preacher and commentator; founder of Va'ad HaYeshivot in Israel

Spinoza Baruch (Benedict) Spinoza (1632–73), Dutch philosopher and exponent of pantheism

Sprinzak Joseph Sprinzak (1885–1959), a founder of Tze'ire Zion; member of Zionist Congresses; co-founder of Hitahadut; executive of Keren HaYesod, Po'ale Zion, Histadrut; 1st speaker of the Knesset

Stampfer Joshua Stampfer (1852–1908), early settler (Petah Tikva); advocate of political Zionism

Stern see **Ya'ir**

Straus Nathan Straus (1848–1931), American merchant and philanthropist (health centres in Jerusalem and Tel Aviv); president of American Jewish Congress

Sturman Hayyim Sturman (1891–1938), pioneer, active in HaShomer and Haganah

Suleiman Sultan Suleiman "the Magnificent" (1496?–1566), conqueror (Belgrade, Budapest, Rhodes, Baghdad, Aden, Algiers) and outstanding administrator, built the present walls of Jerusalem

Suleiman
"the Magnificent"

Syrkin Nachman Syrkin (1868–1924), leader in Hoveve Zion; ideological founder of socialist Zionism; orator and writer for Labour Zionism

Szenes Hannah Szenes (1921–44), poet ("Blessed is the Match") and patriot, killed by Nazis while on a parachute mission

Szold Henrietta Szold (1860–1945), writer and editor; founder of Hadassah; leader in Zionist Executive, Va'ad Leumi, Youth Aliyah

Szold Centre of Applied Sciences, Hebrew Univ. named for Robert Szold (b. 1889), American Zionist leader (ZOA); leader in Jewish Agency, Jewish National Fund

At-Tabari Abu Ja'far Muhammed at-Tabari (839–923), Muslim historian and Koranic scholar, author of a history of the world (*The Annals*)

Tabenkin Yitzhak Tabenkin (1887–1971), Israel labour leader; a founder of HaKibbutz HaMe'uhad, Ahdut HaAvoda; member of Knesset

Tabib Abraham Tabib (1889–1950), head of Yemenite community in Israel; member of Knesset

Tahon Jacob Tahon (1880–1950), chairman of Va'ad Leumi; director of WZO in Palestine

Taiber Israel Taiber (b. 1894), director of insurance and investment companies

Talmei Yehiel *moshav* S.E. of Ashdod, f. 1949, named for Yehiel Tschlenow (1863–1918), leader in Hoveve Zion, WZO, Jewish National Fund, Zionist Executive

Tal Shahar kibbutz W. of Jerusalem, f. 1948, named for Henry Morgenthau, Jr. (1891–1967), Cabinet member under FDR; leader in UJA, Hebrew University

Tarfon R. Tarfon (1st cent.), *tanna*, leading scholar in Yavneh after destruction of the Temple

Tchernichowsky Saul Tchernichowsky (1875–1943), Hebrew poet and translator; edited Hebrew medical dictionary

Tchernichowsky House, Tel Aviv HQ of Hebrew Writers Association

Teller Israel Teller (1835–1921), Hebrew writer, grammarian and teacher, in Galicia and Rehovot

Tel Mond rural community S.E. of Netanya, f. 1929; see Mond**

Tel Yitzhak kibbutz S. of Netanya, f. 1938, named for Isaac Shteiger, Galician Zionist; location of Massuah, Holocaust teachers school

Tel Yosef kibbutz S.E. of Afula, f. 1921, named for Trumpeldor**

Tiomkin Vladimir Tiomkin (1861–1927), active in Revisionist Zionism

Tirat Tzevi kibbutz near Beit Shean, f. 1937, named for R. Kalischer**

Toledano R. Jacob Moshe Toledano (b. 1880), historian and writer; Sephardic leader and educator in Tiberias

Truman Harry S. Truman (1884–1972), American president who recognized new State of Israel

H. Truman

Truman Institute, Mt. Scopus f. 1968, named for Harry S. Truman**

Trumpeldor Yosef Trumpeldor (1880–1920), pioneer; leader in Revisionist Zionism; fell in defence of Tel Hai settlement

Tzefania see **Zephaniah**

Tzidkiyahu see **Zedekiah**

Tzur Jacob Tzur (b. 1906), writer and editor; leader in Jewish Agency, Zionist General Council; Israel diplomat

Tzur Moshe *moshav* E. of Netanya, f. 1937, named for Moshe Kopinas, Greek Zionist leader

Ulitzur Avram Ulitzur (1894–1947), economist, a founder of Talpiot sector of Jerusalem

Ussishkin Menahem Mendel Ussishkin (1863–1941), leader in Hoveve Zion, B'ne Moshe, Zionist Congresses, Jewish National Fund

M. Ussishkin

Ussishkin House nature study institute N.E. of Kiriyat Shmona at kibbutz Dan

Uziel R. Ben-Zion Meir Hai Ouziel (1880–1953), Talmudic scholar and writer; Chief Rabbi of Israel; leader in Mizrahi, Va'ad Leumi, Zionist Congresses, Jewish Agency

Uziyahu Biblical Uzziah, for 52 years king of Judah (II Kings 14:21; 15:1,2); rebuilt Elath (II Kings 14:22); strengthened Jerusalem (II Chron. 26:9)

Da Vinci Leonardo da Vinci (1452–1519), Renaissance painter (i.e. The Last Supper, St. Jerome), sculptor; also famous as architect and engineer

Vital R. Hayyim Ben Joseph Vital (1542–1620), authority on Talmud and Kabbala; active in Safad, Jerusalem and Damascus

Vitkin Joseph Vitkin (1876–1912), a leader in the Second Aliyah; issued famous "Call to Youth" (1905)

Volcani Yitzhak Avigdor Elazari-Volcani (1880–1955), leader in HaPo'el HaTza'ir, WZO, Histadrut; professor of agricultural economics in Hebrew University

Volcani Institute of Agricultural Research, Rehovot see **Volcani**

Al-Walid Caliph Abd al-Malik al-Walid, Arab commander of Palestine; builder of El Aksa Mosque (705–715)

Wallach Moshe Wallach (1886–1957), pioneer of medicine in Eretz Israel; founded and directed Sha'arei Zedek Hospital

Wallenberg Raoul Wallenberg (1912–?), Swedish diplomat who rescued Jews in Hungary during WWII; kidnapped by Russians, status unknown

R. Wallenburg

Warburg Otto Warburg (1859–1938), botanist and professor (Hebrew Univ.); leader in WZO, Keren HaYesod; a founder of Bezalel School

Warren's Shaft Charles Warren (1840–1927), conducted archaeological excavations in Jerusalem 1867–70; discovered Ophel wall

Washington George Washington (1732–99), 1st president of the USA

Waterman Wise Youth Hostel, Jerusalem named for James Waterman Wise (b. 1901), American executive and art collector

Wedgwood Josiah Clement Wedgwood (1872–1943), British statesman, Christian supporter of Zionism

Weinshall Jacob Weinshall (b. 1891), medical doctor and writer; chairman of Revisionist Central Committee 1922–28

Weissburg Hayim Weissburg (1892–1959), early settler; delegate to Zionist Congresses

Weizmann Chaim Weizmann (1874–1952), scientist and professor; leader in WZO, founding of Hebrew University, 1st president of Israel

Weizmann Institute of Science, Rehovot named for Chaim Weizmann**

Wingate Orde Wingate (1903–44), British Brig. General, Christian supporter of Zionism

Wingate Institute school of physical education, S. of Netanya; named for O. Wingate**

Wise R. Stephen S. Wise (1874–1949), writer and orator; founder of the Free Synagogue of New York, the Jewish Institute of Religion; a founder and leader in American Jewish Congress, ZOA

Wolffson David Wolffson (1856–1914), businessman, leader in early Zionism (WZO), associate of Herzl and trustee of his effects; Beit David Wolffson on Mt. Scopus campus, Hebrew University, dedicated 1930

D. Wolffsohn

Ya'akov Avinu "Jacob our Father;" covenant confirmed (Gen. 28:13–22; 35:9–15); blessed, his name becomes "Israel" (Gen. 32:28)

Yad Binyamin youth village N.E. of Ashdod, f. 1962, named for B. Mintz**

Yad Hanna *kibbutzim* "A" and "B" E. of Netanya, f. 1950, named for Hannah Szenes**

Yad Harav Herzog Talmudic centre in Jerusalem, f. 1950, named for R. Herzog**

Yad Kennedy see **Kennedy Memorial**

Yad Mordechai kibbutz S. of Ashkelon, f. 1943, named for M. Anielewicz**; centre of heroic resistance during War of Independence; location of Holocaust Museum   143

Yad Natan *moshav* E. of Ashkelon, f. 1953, named for Natan Komoly (1892–1945), Hungarian leader of General Zionism killed by Nazis

Yad Rambam *moshav* S.E. of Ramla, f. 1955, named for Rambam**

Ya'el Biblical Jael, who killed Sisera (Judg. 4:12ff; 5:24ff)

Yaffe see **Jaffe**

Ya'ir underground name of Abraham Stern (1907–42), active in Haganah, then founder of Lohamei Herut Israel; killed in fight vs. British Palestine authority

A. Stern

Yalag popular name for Y.L. Gordon**

Yannai Alexander Yannai (103–76 B.C.E.), Maccabean ruler and High Priest who governed the Hasmonean kingdom at its greatest expanse

Yavetz pen name of R. Jacob Emden (1697–1776), Kabbalist and *halakhic* authority

Yedidya *moshav* near Netanya, f. 1935, named for Philo (Yedidya) of Alexandria (fl. early 1st cent.), Jewish philosopher and statesman

Yehezkel see **Ezekiel**

Yehi'am kibbutz E. of Nahariya, f. 1946, named for Yehiam Weiz (d. 11 June 1946), killed in struggle with British Mandate authorities ("Night of the Bridges")

Yehoshua Bin Nun Joshua, son of Nun, leader of the Hebrews after Moses (Num. 27:18–23)

Yehuda Biblical Judah, son of Jacob (Gen. 35:23)

Yehuda Halevi R. Judah Halevi (1085?–1140), poet and philosopher (*Sefer HaKuzari*); in warfare of Muslims and Christians in Spain, looked to return to Zion as only hope for Jews

Yehuda Hamaccabi Judah Maccabee, Hasmonean ruler and High Priest 165–160 B.C.E.

Yehuda Hanasi R. Judah HaNasi (135?–220?), compiler of the Mishnah, leader of Palestinian Jewish community

Yellin Avinoam Yellin (1900–37), scholar in Hebrew and Arabic; supervisor of schools under the British Mandate

Yellin David Yellin (1864–1941), professor (Hebrew Univ.); leader in Jerusalem communal life (Hebrew Language Academy, Jewish National Library); leader in Hebrew Teachers Association, Va'ad Leumi

Yemin Moshe first sector of Jerusalem residences outside the Old City; named for Sir Moses Montefiore**

Yemin Orde Youth Institute near kibbutz Nir Etzion S. of Haifa, named for Orde Wingate**

Yeshayahu see **Isaiah**

Yeshurun poetic name of Israel (Deut. 32:15)

Yirmiyahu see **Jeremiah**

Yishai Jesse, King David's father (I Sam. 16:11–13)

Yissa Berakha acronym for R. Ya'akov Saul Elishar (1817–1906), Chief Sephardic Rabbi in Jerusalem

Yitzhak Levi R. Levi Isaac Ben Meir of Berdichev (1740–1810), teacher and leader of Hasidic movement

Yoav Joab (10th cent. B.C.E.), King David's commander (II Sam. 8:16)

Yoel Biblical prophet; see book of Joel

Yohanan Ben Zakkai see **Ben Zakkai**

Yohanan Hasandlar R. Johanan HaSandlar (early 2nd cent.), *tanna*, pupil of R. Akiva**

Yohanan Hyrcanus see **Hyrcanus**

Yona Biblical prophet; see book of Jonah

Yonatan Netanyahu day care centre at Mevasseret Yerushalayim, f. 1980, named for Yonatan Netanyahu (Yoni), killed in successful rescue of hostages from Entebbe (1976)

Yoram Yoram Katz (1936–55), youth leader and paratrooper, killed near Lake Kinneret in battle with Syrians

Yosef Hamelech Joseph, son of Jacob and Rachel (Gen. 30:24), advisor to Pharaoh (Gen. 41ff)

Yossi Ben Yo'ezer Yose Ben Joezer of Zaredah (2nd cent. B.C.E.), head of Sanhedrin in Jerusalem; crucified at time of Hasmonean revolt

Yossi Haglili Yose HaGelili (2nd cent.), scholar and teacher (with R. Akiva**) at Yavneh

Yotam Jotham, king of Judah c. 742–735 B.C.E. (II Kings 15:32–38)

Yunitchman Shimshon Yunitchman (1907–61), medical doctor; member of Betar; member of Knesset

Az-Zahra another name of Fatima, daughter of Muhammed

Zakai David Zakai (b. 1886), astronomer and meteorologist; leader in Histadrut

Zalman Shneur see **Shneur**

Zamenhof Ludwik Lazar Zamenhof (1859–1913), member of Hoveve Zion; inventor of Esperanto

Zangwill Israel Zangwill (1864–1926), Anglo-Jewish novelist; active in Zionist Congresses (for a time leader of "Territorialism")

I. Zangwill

Zebul, Mt. see **Zevulun**

Zechariah prophet during Second Temple period; see book of Zechariah

Zedekiah last king of Judah and Jerusalem 597–586 B.C.E.; appointed by Nebuchadnezzar (II Kings 24:17–18); sought alliance with Egypt (Ezek. 17:11–18) and denounced by prophets Jeremiah and Ezekiel; lost Jerusalem and his sons (Jer. 39:1–10; 52:4–30)

Zeid Alexander Zeid (1886–1938), a pioneer and a founder of HaShomer (1909); discoverer of Beit She'arim necropolis; killed while guarding early settlements

A. Zeid

Zeitlin Hillel Zeitlin (1871–1942), Yiddish writer and editor; Hebrew scholar; killed at Treblinka

Zephaniah Judean prophet; see book of Zephaniah

Zerubavel Jacob (Witkin) Zerubavel (1886–1967), pioneer; author, editor (*Der Yidisher Arbeter, Ha'Ahdut*) and orator; leader in Po'ale Zion, Histadrut, WZO, Jewish Agency

Zevulun Zebulun, son of Jacob (Gen. 30:19–20; 35:23); tribe blessed by Moses (Deut. 33:18–19)

Zichron Ya'akov town S. of Haifa, named for James de Rothschild**

Zichron Yosef Jerusalem suburb, f. 1931, named for Yosef Levi, land agent

Zirelson R. Judah Leib Zirelson (1860–1941), Chief Rabbi of Bessarabia; a founder of Agudat Israel

Zlocisti Theodor Zlocisti (1874–1943), poet and translator, editor; biographer of Moses Hess**·

Zmora Yisrael Zmora (b. 1899), Hebrew writer and editor (*Mahbarot LeSifrut* magazine and publishing house)

Zola Emile Zola (1840–1902), French novelist; champion of Dreyfus**

GLOSSARY

Aggada — sections of the Talmud and Midrash containing stories, illustrations and homiletical expositions

Agudat Israel — world organization of Orthodox Jews, f. 1912 at Kattowitz, Poland: became political party in Israel in 1948

Ahdut Avoda — Zionist Socialist Labour Party in Israel, f. 1919; merged with HaPo'el HaTza'ir in 1930

Aliyah — "ascent" or "going up," applied to immigration of Jews to Israel — a right guaranteed by the Law of Return (1950)

Ashkenazi — literally, "German;" more generally, applied to the Jewish culture of northern and eastern Europe, using Yiddish as vernacular; distinguished from the Sephardic and Oriental Jewish cultures

Betar — abbreviation from B'rit Trumpeldor**; Zionist youth movement founded in 1923 by the Union of Zionist Revisionists; name adopted from the last stronghold of the Bar Kokhba revolt (c. 135 C.E.)

Bilu — abbreviation from Beit Ya'akov Lekhu ve-Nelkhah (Isaiah 2:5); nucleus of the First Aliyah, begun 1882 by Jews from Russia

B'ne Moshe — secret order of Hoveve Zion f. 1889 in Russia under inspiration of Ahad Ha'am**

B'rit Shalom — Peace Association f. 1925 by Arthur Ruppin** and others to foster friendly relations between Arabs and Jews

Caliph — head of the theocracy in Islam, ruling by divine right, usually in hereditary succession

Church — the community of Christians, variously used to refer to all in this generation and in the past, or to a specific denomination, or to a local congregation

Diaspora — the Jews living outside the Land of Israel, especially applied to a) those scattered after the Babylonian exile, b) those scattered at the time of the wars with the Seleucids, Ptolemies and Romans, and c) those remaining outside after the founding of the State of Israel

Ecumene, ecumenical — the worldwide Christian church, especially that section of churches cooperating in the World Council of Churches; used also to apply to the Second Vatican Council (1961–65)

Eretz Israel — the Land of Israel

Etzel — Irgun Zeva'i Le'umi, Jewish underground organization f. 1931 to defend Jewish settlements against Arab marauders; later active in opposition to British Mandate authorities, under command of Menachem Begin from 1943

Exilarch — lay heads of the Jewish community in Babylonia (c. 140–1270 C.E.)

Firman — a decree or authorization issued by a Muslim ruler

Galut — Hebrew for Diaspora

Gaon — title carried by heads of Jewish academies of learning at Sura and Pumbedita in Babylonia (6th–11th cent. C.E.)

Ghetto — urban section set aside for Jewish inhabitants, a restricted area usually enforced by decrees

Habad — Hasidic trend f. by R. Zalman Shneur of Lyady**, emphasizing Torah study; movement headed by Lubavitcher rabbi

Hadassah — women's Zionist organization f. 1912 by Henrietta Szold**

Haganah — underground Jewish defence organization founded after Arab riots of 1920; after World War II active in assisting "illegal" immigration to Eretz Israel; from independence (May, 1948), the regular army of Israel

HaKibbutz HaMe'uhad — union of *kibbutzim* f. 1927 by pioneers of the Third Aliyah

Halakha, halakhic — refers to legal part of Talmud and other Jewish scriptures, especially the written law in the Mishnah and later; codified in Shulhan Arukh of R. Joseph Caro**

HaPo'el — workers' sports organization affiliated with Histadrut, f. 1926

HaPo'el HaMizrahi — religious Zionist movement, f. 1922; with allies, formed the National Religious Party in 1956

HaPo'el HaTza'ir — Labour Party f. 1905 by pioneers of the Second Aliyah; with allies, formed Mapai party in 1929

HaShomer — pioneer self-defence organization of Jewish settlers during the Turkish period, 1909–20

HaShomer HaTza'ir — pioneering movement of Socialist Zionism, f. 1916 in eastern Europe to train youth for kibbutz life in Eretz Israel

Hasidism — popular movement of religious piety launched by Israel Ben Eliezer Ba'al Shem-Tov** (c. 1700–60), healer and charismatic teacher

Haskalah — Jewish involvement in the general movement of Enlightenment in Europe, promoting political emancipation and secular education

HaTikva ("The Hope") — Zionist poem written by N. Imber** (c. 1878), which became Israel's national anthem

HeHalutz — federation of Socialist Zionist youth movements, f. 1915 in USA by David Ben-Gurion** and Y. Ben-Zvi** and in eastern Europe by Joseph Trumpeldor**

Hibbat Zion ("Love of Zion") — movement f. 1882 in Russia to stimulate Jewish awakening and return to Eretz Israel; produced the First Aliyah (Bilu)

Histadrut — General Federation of Workers in Israel, f. 1920; extensive economic activities include cooperatives, social services, industrial and agricultural programs, youth activities, sports, etc.

Hitahadut — Socialist Zionist Party, f. 1920; joined Po'ale Zion to found Ihud Olami in 1932

Holocaust — mass destruction of European Jewry under the Nazi Third Reich

Holy Land — term of religious reference to Eretz Israel, generally used by Christians

Holy Places — term applied to shrines of Jews, Christians and Muslims in Eretz Israel, with access protected by the Israel government after 1967

Hoveve Zion — adherents of Hibbat Zion

I.D.F. ("Zahal") — Israel Defence Forces, established in 1948 as successor to the Haganah

Ihud — society to promote Arab–Jewish amity, f. 1942 by J.L. Magnes**

Irgun (Irgun Zeva'i Le'umi) — see **Etzel**

Kabbala, Kabbalist — refers to mystical, esoteric tradition in Judaism, especially as developed in the 12th century and later; a major centre after the expulsion of Jewish teachers from the Iberian peninsula (1492–96) was developed in Safad*

Keren HaYesod — financial arm of WZO, f. 1920, supporting colonization in Eretz Israel

Kibbutz, kibbutzim (pl.) — collective communities, with common ownership of property, means of production, joint purchasing and marketing

Knesset — parliament of Israel, with several political parties

KZ — concentration camp in the Nazi empire

Lehi (Lohamei Herut Israel, "Stern Group") — armed underground group, f. 1940 in breakaway from the Irgun

Mapai — Israel Labour Party, f. 1930 under leadership of David Ben-Gurion**

Mapam — Labour Zionist Party in Israel, f. 1948

Marrano — term applied to Jews who officially converted to Christianity during persecutions of 1492–96 in Iberian peninsula

Midrash, midrashic — a method of interpretation; chiefly used to refer to rabbinic commentaries and exegesis both scriptural and sermonic (c. 70–1000 C.E.)

Minaret — slender tower of a Muslim mosque, from which a crier (*muazzin*) issues call to prayer 5 times daily

Mishnah — codification and redaction of Jewish law, especially that arranged by R. Yehuda Hanasi**

Mizrahi — religious Zionist movement, f. 1902; merged with National Religious Party, 1955

Moshav, moshavim (pl.) — cooperative communities, usually with collective production and private consumption, frequently built upon national lands

Mosque — a Muslim place of worship

Musar — late 19th century movement associated with *yeshivot* in Lithuania; taught strict ethical behaviour in line with *halakhic* precepts

Nagid — head of Jewish community in Muslim and some Christian areas in the Middle Ages

Palestine — a correct term for Eretz Israel for the years when the land was a province of the Roman Empire and for the years of the British Mandate (1920–48)

Palmach — volunteer striking force of the Haganah, f. 1941 by Yitzhak Sadeh**; merged with I.D.F. in 1948

PICA — society founded by Baron Edmond de Rothschild** to promote colonization (1924–57), taking over from ICA founded in 1891 by Baron Maurice de Hirsch**

Po'ale Zion — Socialist Zionist movement; World Union f. 1907 by Ber Borochov** and others; split later into several factions

Revisionists — movement f. 1925 and led by V. Jabotinsky**; strong advocates of political Zionism

Sanhedrin — supreme council of the Jews in Eretz Israel under Roman occupation

Sephardic, Sephardim — refers to Jews descended from those expelled from Spain and Portugal (1492–96), distinct from Ashkenazi, using Ladino rather than Yiddish

Shtetl — Jewish village in E. Europe, originally in the Pale of Settlement in Russian Poland (1791–1917)

Sultan — a Muslim ruler, especially in the former Ottoman Turkish Empire

Synagogue — a building for Jewish public prayer which became the focus of Jewish communal life in the Diaspora

Talmud, Talmudist — refers to commentaries of the teachers on the Mishnah; Jerusalem Talmud completed c. 500 C.E. in Tiberias and other centres of learning in Eretz Israel; the Babylonian Talmud, completed c. 500 C.E. in the academies of that empire, has enjoyed greater popularity and influence

Tanna, tannaim (pl.) — Jewish sages (c. 20–200 C.E.) who produced the Mishnah and led the people during the traumas of the destruction of the Temple, the defeat of national hopes in Bar Kokhba's revolt, and the growing alienation between Jews and Christians

Technion — Institute of Technology opened in Haifa* in 1924

Tel ("mound") — a hill or hillock built up by human beings over the centuries, with successive levels of the remains of settlements; in the modern period perhaps the site of an archaeological "dig"

Tora va Avoda ("Torah and Labour") — program of Mizrahi youth, f. 1925

UJA — United Jewish Appeal, f. 1939 as chief agency soliciting funds for Jewish institutions and programs

Va'ad Leumi — National Council of the Jews of Palestine under the British Mandate (1920–48)

Wadi — Arab name for a ravine or coulee, usually dry except for rushing water or floods during occasional rains

WIZO — Women's International Zionist Organization, f. 1920; 50 federations throughout the world except for USA, where Hadassah has functioned since 1912

WZO — World Zionist Organization, f. 1897 on initiative of Theodor Herzl** at the First Zionist Congress

Yeshiva, yeshivot (pl.) — name of institutes of Talmudic learning, used since the flowering of learning in Eretz Israel and Babylonia (c. 70–500 C.E.)

Yishuv — the Jewish community in Eretz Israel prior to the formation of the State (1948)

Youth Aliyah — Zionist program for rescue of Jewish children and educating them in Eretz Israel; f. 1932 and headed by Henrietta Szold**

Zealots — Jewish resistance fighters against the Roman occupation, known in the time of Jesus of Nazareth and especially prominent in the war of 66–73 C.E.

Zionism — movement with goal of returning Jews to Eretz Israel; term coined in 1890 by N. Birnbaum**

ZOA — Zionist Organization of America, f. 1898